D1276734

ISRAEL AT
40

ISRAEL AT
40

Julian J. Landau

WELLFLEET
PRESS

Concept and layout   *Georgette Corcos*

Editor   *Shlomo Ketko*

Copyright © 1988 by G.G. The Jerusalem Publishing House Ltd.,
Jerusalem.

Published by
THE WELLFLEET PRESS
A Division of BOOK SALES, INC.
110 Enterprise Avenue
Secaucus, New Jersey 07094

All rights reserved. No part of this publication may be reproduced or transmitted in any form or by any means, electronic or mechanical, including photo-
copying, recording or any information storage or retrieval system, without
prior written permission from the copyright owner.

All North American rights reserved by William S. Konecky Associates, Inc.,
New York, N.Y. 10011

ISBN: 1-55521-203-4

Printed in Israel
Typeset, printed and bound by Keterpress Enterprises Jerusalem
Planned and produced by The Jerusalem Publishing House

Contents

Introduction

ISRAEL AT 40 is the exciting story of the Jewish state, a modern democracy whose history has its roots in remote biblical times. It is the story of Zionism, the yearning to return to Zion which brought a people back from exile to their ancient homeland. It is the saga of the birth and building of a state after centuries of foreign rule.

ISRAEL AT 40 vividly describes the country's geography and its society, its cities and its institutions, health and welfare services, education and culture, and its foreign relations. It explains how a denuded land has been made to flourish, how the Jewish people and the Zionist Movement created the conditions for founding a state, and how the population welcomed and absorbed twice its number of Holocaust survivors and refugees.

ISRAEL AT 40 portrays the people of Israel in all their variety of origin and describes how they live. It depicts their struggle for survival in the face of continuing hostility and warfare. It records their difficulties and accomplishments, their democratic way of life, their successes in closing the gap between "haves" and "have nots", and their relations with the other nations of the world.

Lavishly illustrated, ISRAEL AT 40 is the dramatic account of a nation searching for peace, of the rebuilding of an ancient land, whose past continues to be unearthed and brought to life in the context of modern times.

Acknowledgments

The Publishers wish to express their gratitude to the following institutions for the use of photographs from their archives: Beth Ha-Tefutsoth, Tel Aviv; Central Zionist Archives; Government Press Office; Ha'aretz Museum, Tel Aviv; Hadassah Medical Organization; Haifa Tourism Development Association; Israel Department of Antiquities and Museums; Israel Museum, Jerusalem; Kvuzat Geva; Ministry of Education and Culture; Ministry of Health; Ministry of Tourism; Police Headquarters; Technion, Haifa; Tel Aviv Municipality; Wingate Institute of Physical Culture; and the following photographers: Azariah Alon; Moshe Caine; David Harris; N. Garo; Zev Radovan; A. van der Heyden.

Jacket illustrations *Photos: Israel Museum (front top); David Harris (front bottom); Government Press Office (back)*

In view of the large number of illustrations included in this volume, the Publishers wish to apologise in advance for any involuntary omissions and invite persons or bodies concerned to write to the Publishers.

Opposite page:
The Menorah *(candelabrum)*
which stands opposite the
Knesset. On the seven branches
are depicted in relief the princi-
pal figures and events which
mark the history of the Jewish
people.

(left)
Declaration of Independence of
the State of Israel.

ISRAEL AT 40

Digging up the past

*Opposite page
(clockwise from left)
Seal depicting a man harvesting
with a sickle (Hecht Museum,
University of Haifa); clay figures
of a woman bathing, and of a
woman kneading dough, found
at the Phoenician cemetery at
Achzib, dated to the 8th century
BCE; Iron-Age earthenware
figurine of a harp player found at
Ashdod; Phoenician clay figure of
a woman playing the cymbals
from the 7th century BCE (Israel
Museum); detail of a pottery
incense stand showing a figure
playing the double pipe, c. 1000
BCE, from Ashdod (Israel
Museum).*

*Ivory figurines of the Chalcolithic
period from the region south of
Beersheba. (Israel Museum)*

To Israelis, archeology is not only, as the word is defined, the "knowledge of the ancient," it is more than just a study of the past, more than an excursion into the history of the people who lived on the land, and more than an examination of the ruins of centuries gone by, it is a fascinating preoccupation.

The real meaning of archeology to all Israelis — young and old, veteran and newcomer — was best explained by one of its well-known devotees, the late Moshe Dayan. In his autobiography Dayan describes how he decided to explore Nahal Beersheba, a wadi in the Negev, the day after he returned to civilian life in 1974. Discovering a prehistoric cave, he lowered himself into it by a rope tied to the bumper of his car. Once inside, he discerned a hearth, the remains of pots, and utensils: "I crouched by the ancient hearth. It was as though the fire had only just died down, and I did not need to close my eyes to conjure up the woman of the house bending over to spark its embers into flame as she prepared the meal for her family. My family."

Thus, the fascination that Israelis have for each new dig, for each artifact that is uncovered, and for each wall or building that remains from the time of their ancestors, is a search for their roots, a desire to know their people better — how they lived and worshipped, how they built and travelled, how they ate and dressed, how they worked, played, painted and beautified themselves.

Modern Research

Modern archeological exploration of the Holy Land began for similar reasons — the search by Western scholars for the roots of their Christian heritage. This revival of interest in the Middle East as the earliest center of civilization is today more than two hundred and fifty years old. It coincided with the renewed political interest of Europe in the region during the 18th century. Bishop R. Pococke, among others, visited Palestine in 1738 and wrote a comprehensive description of the country's antiquities. Sixty years later, Napoleon took French scholars with him on his military expedition to Egypt and Palestine and the resulting *Description de l'Egypte*, published in 1803–13, included a detailed description of the Holy Land.

Modern topographical research, specifically emphasizing the location of historic and holy sites in the country, which laid the foundations for subsequent archeological explorations, was inaugurated by Edward Robinson. A professor of Bible at the New York Theological Seminary, Robinson first visited the Holy Land in 1824, travelling throughout the country and using scientific methods — topographic observations, Semitic philology, and biblical and historical data — to identify hundreds of biblical sites. He found the remains of a stairway,

near the southwestern corner of the Western Wall, now known as Robinson's Arch, identified Josephus' Third Wall of Jerusalem, and discovered the fortified castle of Masada, constructed above the Dead Sea by King Herod in 37-31 BCE.

Robinson was followed by other topographers in whose footsteps came the archeologists. The first of these was the French orientalist

Lion hunt depicted on a mosaic floor of the Byzantine period at Beth-Shean.

Men treading grapes shown on a Byzantine period mosaic floor at Beth-Shean.

Felicien de Saulcy, who uncovered the so-called Tomb of the Kings in Jerusalem. But de Saulcy was more influenced by theory than by fact and mistakenly insisted that the tombs were those of the descendants of King David, when they are actually the royal tombs of the Kings of Adiabene.

In 1865 a more serious effort was organized in the Jerusalem Room of London's Westminster Cathedral. Under the direction of the Archbishop of York and with the backing of the British Secret Service (who felt that they could obtain accurate military reports under a scientific cover), the Palestine Exploration Fund was born. That same year the PEF's first expedition — composed, as were subsequent missions, of members of Her Majesty's Armed Forces and the Royal Engineers —

came to map and survey the Holy Land, particularly Jerusalem. It was led by Charles Wilson, who discovered another huge arch (Wilson's Arch) which formed part of the bridge leading to the upper city, prepared an ordinance survey of Jerusalem, and planned the work of the expeditions which were to follow.

Two years later the brilliant young Lieutenant Charles Warren led the second PEF mission to Palestine. Unable to obtain permission from the Turkish authorities to dig within the Temple Mount esplanade, Warren, an engineer, dug narrow shafts deep into the ground, turning at right angles to the bedrock, until he reached the walls of the Mount. The resulting finds were often mistakenly dated, but the extraordinary quality and scope of his work stood as a landmark in exploration for many years. Warren's monumental *Survey of Western Palestine*, conducted between 1871 and 1878 and written with Claude Conder, was the first systematic mapping of the country and has since provided a sound basis for all archeological research in the country.

But it was not only careful systematic exploration which yielded the

Wilson's Arch, beside the Western Wall. Today it serves as a synagogue.

The Siloam Inscription. It describes how King Hezekiah's tunnel was dug by two teams of miners starting at opposite ends, working toward each other and meeting in the middle.

important discoveries, chance was also an element. The Moabite Stone or Mesha Stela, which contains an account of the warfare between Moab and Israel described in the Bible, was accidentally found in 1868. In 1880 the Siloam Inscription was inadvertently uncovered on the wall of Hezekiah's tunnel in Jerusalem detailing King Hezekiah's digging a tunnel to bring the water from the Pool of Siloam to the city of Jerusalem.

(left)
Remains of Qasrin synagogue in the Golan.

Seat carved out of a single basalt stone in the form of an armchair, found at Chorazin in Upper Galilee.

Opposite page:
Philistine pottery pitcher painted with geometrical designs and birds. The Philistines appeared in the area at the end of the Late Bronze Age and came into frequent conflict with the Israelites. Remains of their culture, mainly pottery, from the 12th and 11th centuries BCE have been found at many sites on the coastal plain.

Canaanite cultic stand of the 10th century BCE found at Taanach, a short distance from Megiddo. An interesting motif of decoration on the second register is the stylized tree of life flanked by two goats nibbling at it. Extensive excavations at the site of biblical Taanach revealed remains dating from the Early Bronze Age to the Arab period.

It was, however, in 1890 that scientific Palestinian archeology really began when Flinders Petrie, Professor of Egyptology at University College in London, excavated Tell el-Hesi, some 25 km. (16 miles) southeast of Gaza. Petrie carefully and accurately recorded the level at which each artifact was found, and showed how different fragments made it possible to date the various strata of the mound, thereby establishing the chronology of occupation and habitation. He was rightly called the "Father of Palestinian Archeology."

Before the turn of the century other archeological societies were founded, including the German Palestinian Society (1877), the French School of Biblical and Archeological Studies (1890), and the American School of Oriental Research (1900).

An important survey of ancient synagogues in Galilee was made by German and Austrian Bible scholars and architects in 1905–7. This survey is still a basic work for the study of the ancient synagogues in the Holy Land.

Excavations were carried out by one of Petrie's students, R.A.S. Macalister, at Gezer (1902–9), one of the six most important cities in the country throughout the last three millennia BCE, strategically situated at the junction of the Via Maris in the Judean foothills. Further excavations were made during this period at Megiddo (1903–5), an important Canaanite city in the north of Palestine; at Jericho (1901–9), one of the oldest fortified cities in the ancient Near East, north of the Dead Sea, known from the biblical account of how the walls of the city, surrounded by the Israelites led by Joshua, fell at the sound of trumpets.

A turning point in the archeology of Palestine was brought about by an American expedition sent by Harvard University which during 1908 and 1910–11 excavated the biblical Samaria (Shomron), capital of the Kingdom of Israel. The expedition's greatest contribution to modern archeology was the introduction of methodological ways of excavating and of handling finds.

Under the British Mandate
After the First World War excavations were resumed and intensified under British rule. The most outstanding of those who explored the

(bottom left)
Clay anthropomorphic jar of the Middle Bronze Age from Jericho.

(bottom right)
Excavations showing fortifications at ancient Jericho.

Stone tower in the town wall of ancient Jericho dating back to the 10th-8th millennia BCE.

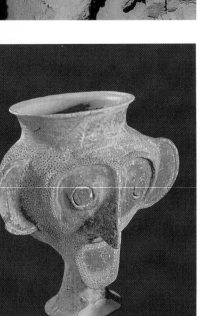

Dagger and javelin heads dating from the 2nd millennium BCE from Jericho.

Holy Land during the next two decades was W. F. Albright, who came to Palestine under the auspices of the Department of Antiquities which was established by the Mandatory Government. Albright headed the American School for Oriental Research. He had a gift for stratigraphy (the careful examination of each stratum of the dig), and his meticulous excavation of Tell Beit-Mirsim (1926–32), southwest of Hebron, helped establish pottery sequence on a scientific foundation.

(left)
Standing stones on a Bronze Age Canaanite "high place" used for cultic purposes at Gezer.

Gold figure of the goddess Astarte dating from the 14th century BCE, found at Gezer.

Major excavations were carried out at Beth-She'an (1921–28) where a sequence of 5,000 years of history was traced; further digs at Megiddo (1925–39); at Samaria (1931–35) by a joint expedition of American and British institutions, together with the Hebrew University; at Jericho by the Department of Antiquities on behalf of the British School of Archeology in Jerusalem; and at Lachish (1932–36), one of the central cities in the coastal plain, whose king was one of the five who fought Joshua and were beaten by the Israelites. All these excavations added a great deal to existing knowledge of the pre-biblical and biblical periods. Finds were placed in the Palestine Archeological Museum in Jerusalem and the results published in scores of volumes.

A remarkable excavation during this period was carried out under the direction of the doyen of Israeli archeologists, Benjamin Mazar, on behalf of the Hebrew University and the Israel Exploration Society at Beth-Shearim (1936–40). This large Jewish town which was the seat of

(clockwise from left)
Part of the excavation area at Hazor.
Megiddo: Remains of storehouses or barracks from King Ahab's time; ivory horn with gold bands, made from an elephant's tusk, from the late Bronze Age. It was filled with oil and used for anointing; aerial view of the excavations.

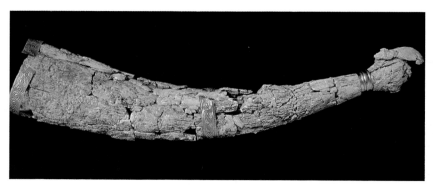

the Sanhendrin (Jewish Supreme Council) in the 2nd century CE, with its necropolis, is situated on the southern slopes of the mountains of Lower Galilee, facing the Jezreel Valley.

The Second World War and the battles preceding Israel's independence stilled the spades of the archeologists. Nevertheless, it was during this period that one of the most exciting discoveries of recent times was made, again by chance. In the spring of 1947 two Bedouin searching for a stray goat on the cliffs that border the northwest shore of the Dead Sea, accidentally came upon a cave where they found seven elongated cylindrical jars containing decaying rolls of leather. The scrolls eventually made their way, through a Syrian shoemaker in Bethlehem and the Metropolitan of the Assyrian Church in Jerusalem, to the American School of Oriental Research and the Department of Antiquities to the Hebrew University. Both Professor Albright and Professor E. L. Sukenik (of the Hebrew University) realized that these were the most ancient copies in existence of various books of the Bible and the Apocrypha written in Hebrew script and contained first-hand information about daily life in the first and second centuries BCE. Eventually many of the scrolls came into Israeli hands and are exhibited in the Shrine of the Book at the Israel Museum in Jerusalem.

The caves of Qumran, where the Dead Sea Scrolls were found.

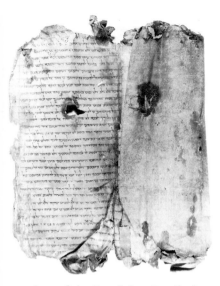

One of the Dead Sea Scrolls from the Qumran Caves, before being opened.

Israeli Archeologists

When the War of Independence ended, work resumed, this time led by a new generation of Israeli scholars who followed in the footsteps of their predecessors. At first the excavations were concentrated at sites which were endangered by the rapid expansion of the country, such as that at Tell Qasile, the 12th century BCE Philistine settlement on the northern bank of the Yarkon River in Tel Aviv. However in the 1950s and 1960s a series of large-scale digs were undertaken throughout the country.

In the Qumran area, where the Dead Sea Scrolls had been discovered, a number of expeditions were launched in the early 1950s which uncovered evidence of settlement in the Chalcolithic period. In 1960–61 a survey was made of the entire area between Masada and Ein Gedi. During the search Professor Yigael Yadin (Chief-of-Staff and Cabinet Minister) uncovered a cave with letters written by Shimon Bar-Kochba, who led the revolt against Rome in 132–135 CE. This was followed, in 1963–65, by Yadin's thorough excavation of Masada which uncovered the entire complex built by Herod in 37 BCE as a retreat for his family, and shed much light on the period during which the fortress was occupied and held until 73 CE by the Zealots in their war against Rome.

The prehistoric periods in Palestine have been excavated by a number of archeologists. For example, at Tel Ubadiya, near Afikim in the Jordan Valley, anthropoid remains were unearthed, dating back to 300,000–600,000 BCE, together with fossil bones of elephants, rhinoceros, hippopotamus and catfish. Mousterian skeletons, kin to the Neanderthal Man, were found in the Galilee and on Mt. Carmel. Flint tools of early Paleolithic origin were also discovered on the Carmel as well as in the Judean Desert, while Natufian skeletons of the Mesolithic age have come to light in Jericho.

Camels in the Negev.

The expedition at Hazor (1955–58) led by Yigael Yadin on behalf of the Hebrew University, opened up a new era of archeological activity in Israel. In this excavation the younger generation of Israeli archeologists, all of whom received their training at the Hebrew University, took part in uncovering the large Canaanite city in Upper Galilee, conquered by Joshua and later built up by Solomon.

Other expeditions uncovered a city which existed for some 1,700 years, from the Bronze Age to the Byzantine period at Ashdod (1962), one of the main Philistine cities in the Judean Plain; an Israelite Temple and various industries from the Judean monarchy at the eastern Negev city of Arad (1962–65); the Nabatean, Roman and Byzantine cities of Avdat in the central Negev (1958–60); a monumental city gate of the Israelite period at Tel Dan (begun in 1966 by the Israel Department of Antiquities and Museums and still proceeding under the auspices of the Hebrew Union College — Jewish Institute of Religion); remains of a Roman theater as well as Byzantine churches and a mar-

Clay mask of the Canaanite period from Hazor.

(left)
Excavations at Hazor.

(left)
View of the fortress at the site of biblical Arad.

Satyr-head ornamentation on a Hellenistic pottery brazier from Dor, north of Caesarea.

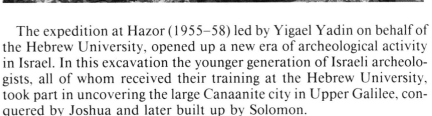

Capital of column decorated with a menorah *(seven-branched candelabrum) from an ancient synagogue at Caesarea.*

(top right)
Aerial view of the Roman theater at Caesarea.

(bottom right)
Portico of the synagogue at Eshtamoa.

Hoard of silver scrap, dross and jewelry from the Israelite period, found at Eshtamoa.

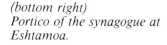

ket at Caesarea (1959–63), capital of the Roman province of Judea for about six hundred years; and a variety of Jewish synagogues dating from the fourth to the seventh centuries throughout the Galilee.

After the Six Day War
Many of the sites that have become accessible to Israeli archeologists have been explored. On the Golan Heights, remains have been found from the Chalcolithic era, dating back some 6,000 years, as well as evidence of intensive Jewish settlement during the first centuries of the Common Era. A number of synagogues, churches, and monasteries of the early Christian period have been partially restored. In the Sinai Desert numerous sites were explored and excavations carried out in Samaria, the Judean Hills, and near Hebron where the ancient synagogue at Eshtamoa was uncovered and restored.

Jerusalem has always fascinated scholars and was explored in the pre-State period by expeditions sponsored by the Rothschild Mission

previous page:
(clockwise from top)
Ivory carving from King Ahab's palace in Samaria; Samaritan sarcophagi of the Roman period from Shechem; stone Mezuza of the early Byzantine period, from Samaria (Israel Museum).

(the first Jewish archeological expedition to the Holy Land), the Palestine Exploration Fund and later the Israel Exploration Society. A large fortress from the end of the Judean monarchy was found at Ramat Rachel (1959–62), and Jerusalem has been extensively explored by Kathleen Kenyon from 1961 to 1967.

Mosaic floor of the synagogue at Ein Gedi.

Capital in "proto-Aeolian" style, dating from the period of the last kings of Judah, found at Ramat Rachel.

Clay seals from the end of the Judean Kingdom found at the City of David in Jerusalem, bearing personal names from that period (City of David Excavations).

General view of the City of David excavations, looking north.

Aerial view of excavations along the southern side of the Temple Mount area in Jerusalem, looking west.

Restored section of the Cardo.

The excavations by Mazar and Ben-Dov on the southern slopes of the Temple Mount (which began in 1968) have revealed huge Umayyad palaces, as well as shedding light on the period of the Second Temple. In the Jewish Quarter, Nahman Avigad (beginning in 1969) has uncovered remnants of the First Temple period, the "burnt house" destroyed by the Romans when they captured Jerusalem in 70 CE, the Nea Church built by Emperor Justinian in 543 CE, and segments of the Cardo, the Roman thoroughfare which has now been reconstructed and refurbished. Remains from the Second Temple, the Byzantine, Arab, Crusader and Turkish periods have been discovered in the Citadel near the Armenian Quarter, in Zahal Square and on Mt. Zion. Excavations of the ancient City of David by the late Dr. Yigal Shiloh from 1978 to 1987 have produced finds from the Jebusite and early Monarchy periods.

One of the most exciting recent finds in Jerusalem was made at Ketef Hinnom at the junction of the Jerusalem–Bethlehem roads. One of the caves was found intact with many metal, ivory and glass objects, coins, pottery vessels and silver and gold jewelry. Among the outstanding items are two small cylindrical silver plaques rolled up into tiny scrolls dating to the 7th century BCE. Engraved in the metal was a text almost identical with the biblical verses of the Priestly Blessing, written in ancient Hebrew script — the most ancient biblical text found yet.

Many of the sites mentioned above have been reconstructed or cleared and opened to the public. The National Parks Authority has established dozens of archeological parks, and important finds have been made available for public viewing. Those discoveries not left on the site are displayed in the country's more than 20 local and national museums, especially the Israel Museum in Jerusalem.

Thus archeology in the Holy Land has uncovered much of the history of man, putting on display the life and times of centuries of habitation, numerous peoples and rulers, different religions and ways of worship, and endless styles of living and building — all an integral part of the history of the Land and the People of Israel.

Burial caves at Ketef Hinnom, Jerusalem.

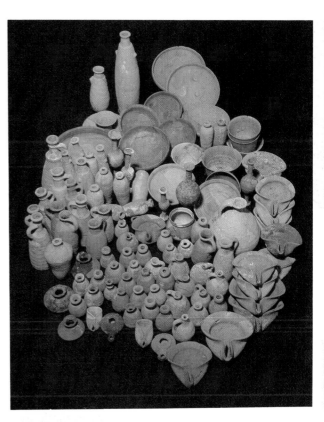

Pottery assemblage from the 7th-6th centuries BCE found in one of the burial caves at Ketef Hinnom. (Israel Museum)

(top left and center)
Silver plaque of the 7th century BCE, bearing a fragment of the Priestly Blessing, found rolled up as a cylinder scroll at Ketef Hinnom. (Israel Museum)

Burial cave complex with burial niches of the First Temple period in the grounds of the Monastery of St. Etienne in Jerusalem.

(left and right)
Stone headrest for the deceased on a burial bench at St. Etienne and two of the elaborate burial chambers arranged one behind the other.

A young state with 4000 years of history

The bond between the Jewish people and the Land of Israel goes back nearly 4,000 years. It is a bond which began with the origin and birth of the Jews. It has never been broken, except in a physical sense — by conquest and exile — over the centuries in which the people tenaciously held on to their religion, beliefs and common origin.

It was in the Land of Israel that the national identity of the Jewish

The sacrifice of Isaac depicted on the mosaic pavement of the ancient synagogue of Beth Alpha, dated to the early 6th century. On the right side, Abraham is shown holding a knife; Isaac appears to the right of Abraham with his hands tied behind his back.

People was formed. It was here that their religion was molded, crystalized and proclaimed. From here their message of a universal God, the brotherhood of all men, justice and peace, went out to the world.

Despite invaders, conquerors and foreign rulers, the Jewish People maintained a physical presence in the Land of Israel since the time of the Bible. Those who were exiled and forced to live elsewhere kept the Land, Zion and Jerusalem at the center of their hopes, prayers and daily lives, until the renaissance of the Jewish State of Israel, in 1948, saw the realization of their dreams.

The Biblical Period
In the Middle Bronze Age, around the 17th century BCE, the Patriarch Abraham left Ur of the Chaldees (an ancient city in Babylonia) at God's command, and went to the Promised Land. In return for Abraham's recognition of the One God, he was promised that his descendants would inherit the Land.

It was to the Patriarch Jacob that both the Land and the People owed their name. Because he strove with God and men and prevailed, Jacob was told that his name henceforth would be Israel. His sons became the Children of Israel, as did their descendants for centuries to come, and their homeland became the Land of Israel.

The edifice over the Cave of Machpelah at Hebron.

Slavery in Egypt, to where Jacob and his sons had fled from famine in the Land, the Exodus from Egypt, wandering in the desert under the leadership of Moses, which took place around the 13th century BCE, were the crucible which forged the People of Israel into a nation. As they conquered the land of Canaan, the Children of Israel slowly transformed their nomadic way of life, establishing permanent settlements.

In the face of the continued threat to Israel by the Philistines, the leadership of the Judges (among whom Deborah, Gideon and Samson in particular) was replaced by Saul, the first King of Israel (1020 BCE). Under Saul's successor, King David, the tribes were unified, and Jerusalem became the capital of the united nation which had become a major political and economic factor in the area.

David's son, Solomon (970–930 BCE), ruled over an empire which

(left)
The tablets of the Law carved in stone.

Moses standing on top of the flaming Mount Sinai holding the tablets of the Law. To his left stands Joshua, and the Israelites encircle the mountain. From the 14th-century illuminated Sarajevo Haggadah. (Sarajevo National Museum)

Solomon passing judgement over the two women, shown on an illuminated manuscript of the 13th century. (British Museum)

(right)
Samuel anointing David, who stands with his hands folded. Wall painting from Dura-Europos synagogue on the Euphrates River, dated to the 3rd century.

stretched from the Euphrates to Egypt. He built the Temple in Jerusalem, making the city the spiritual center of the nation and the People for centuries to come. After Solomon's death the kingdom was divided into Judah and Israel. The Kingdom of Israel, in the north, with the capital Samaria, was conquered by the Assyrians in 722 BCE and the inhabitants were deported. The Kingdom of Judah lasted another 150 years until it was also conquered in 586, the Temple destroyed and the inhabitants exiled to Babylon.

Judean captives driven out of the destroyed city of Lachish. From a relief from Nineveh.

During much of this period, a unique group of men — the Prophets of Israel — who served either as advisors to the kings or as their critics, raised their voices in utterings and exhortations. Isaiah, Jeremiah, Amos and Ezekiel spoke to the kings and to the People of Israel and Judah in the Land of Israel, but their words are as appropriate today as they were centuries ago.

Hellenistic, Hasmonean and Roman Rule

For fifty years the Babylonian exiles longed for their homeland until Cyrus, King of Persia, conquered the Babylonian Empire (in 538 BCE), and issued a declaration which allowed the Jews to return to Jerusalem. The returnees rebuilt the Temple and, despite the overthrow of the Persian Empire by Alexander the Great, the conquest by the Ptolemies (Egyptians) and Seleucids (Syrians), the Jews practiced their religion unhindered and generally conducted their own affairs for the next 350 years. When King Antiochus sought to prohibit Jewish religious practices and force idol worship in the Temple, the people rose in revolt and led by the Hasmonean Judah the Maccabee, defeated the Hellenistic armies in 164 BCE (a victory still commemorated by the festival of Hanukah).

During the century that followed, the Hasmonean kingdom flourished and the nation's borders expanded. But a war of succession brought in the Romans, who severely limited the autonomy of the Hasmoneans. In 37 BCE the Romans appointed Herod as King of Judea. During his 33 year reign, Herod ruled the country tyrannically, but also rebuilt and enlarged the Temple in Jerusalem and constructed cities, fortresses and palaces throughout the land. After his death, the rule of the Roman procurators became increasingly oppressive. In addition to the general enmity toward Roman rule, there were conflicts among the Jews themselves. There was also an increase in the activities of visionaries and prophets who spread messianic expectations among the people. Among these was Jesus of Nazareth who was crucified by the Romans.

Finally the Jews revolted against the Romans, but were defeated, and in 70 CE Titus conquered Jerusalem, destroyed the Second Temple and exiled thousands of Jews. Half a century later, in 132, the Jews, led by Simon Bar Kochba, revolted again. Again they were defeated. The Romans rebuilt Jerusalem, renamed it Aelia Capitolina, and the Land of Israel became the Roman province, Palestina.

Model of the Second Temple based on the reconstruction made by Prof. Avi-Yonah.

Head found in Egypt, believed to represent Herod the Great.

(right)
Aerial view of Herodion, the palace-fortress in the Judean desert built by Herod the Great.

The Byzantine Period

In 324 the character of the Land changed drastically. The Christian emperor Constantine defeated the rulers of the Eastern (Byzantine) Roman Empire and thus conquered Jerusalem and the Holy Land. He saw Christian rule over the Land of Israel as the fulfillment of the Gospels. At the sites holy to Christians throughout the country, magnificent churches were built, including the Church of the Holy Sepulcher in Jerusalem; pilgrims were encouraged to settle in the Holy Land. Despite oppression under the Byzantines, the Jews found strength and comfort in their religious heritage. The sermons of the Rabbis to the people were compiled, and the Jerusalem Talmud, which incorporated discussions that had taken place in the Palestinian academies, was completed.

The Arab Period

In the 7th century, Muhammad gave the inhabitants of the Arabian Peninsula a common religion, Islam. In 638 the Arabs conquered the Land under Caliph Omar and gradually settled it. In 691 Abd al-Malik built the magnificent Dome of the Rock in Jerusalem, on the Temple Mount, which, together with the El Aksa Mosque, became a focal point of the Islamic religion.

The first Muslim-Arab caliphate, the Umayyads, gave way to the Abbasids from Baghdad, then to the Seljuks, a Turkish people who embraced Islam, and they, in turn, to the Fatimids, a militant Arabian dynasty. Some Arab rulers gave the Jews and Christians full religious freedom, but others imposed severe restrictions on both groups.

The Crusader Period

At the end of the 11th century, Pope Urban II issued an appeal to the faithful to recover the holy places for Christianity. Four years later, in 1099, the knights of the First Crusade conquered Jerusalem, massacring its Jewish and Moslem inhabitants.

Although they rebuilt the old churches, the Crusaders remained aloof from the local population and squabbled among themselves. They were defeated by the Egyptian Sultan Saladin in 1187 and again, after renewed Crusades, by Baybars in 1291, when Christian domination of the Holy Land finally ended.

Mameluke and Ottoman Rule

During the two and a quarter centuries of rule by the Mamelukes of Egypt, the Holy Land became a desolate province. Coastal cities, such as Acre and Jaffa, were destroyed in fear of new Crusades; other cities remained in ruins. Heavy taxes forced many to leave the land and plagues and earthquakes added to the misery and poverty.

The conquest of the Holy Land by the Ottoman Turks in 1517 began a period of prosperity and order. Suleiman the Magnificent rebuilt the city walls of Jerusalem, expanded the cultivated lands, brought in new industries, stimulated Jewish immigration, and introduced a secure and organized administration.

But by the end of the 16th century, the Ottoman army lost its strict discipline and its frequent rebellions against the Sultan were reflected

Sultan Suleiman the Magnificent who rebuilt the walls of Jerusalem (1520–66).

(left)
Series of stone archways at the site of the Crusader city of Caesarea.

One of two pairs of lions which flank St. Stephen's Gate, also known as the Lions' Gate, built by Suleiman the Magnificent.

Preceding pages:
(left)
Remains of the Roman forum at Sebaste (Samaria). Herod developed the city and renamed it Sebaste (a Greek form of the Latin name Augustus) in honor of the first Roman emperor.
(right)
Base of the Tower of Phasael. One of three towers built by Herod to strengthen the defenses of his palace in Jerusalem, it was named after his brother.

(right top and bottom)
Remains of the fortified winter palace on the northern shore of the Sea of Galilee of the Umayyad caliph Walid I who ruled from Damascus in the early 8th century CE.

Opposite page:
The citadel of Banias (Qal'at Nimrud), built by the Crusaders in the Hermon Range to guard the vital Damascus route.

Khan (caravanserai) in Acre built in the late 18th century by Jazzar Pasha, the regional governor, as part of a plan to turn the city into the center of trade and commerce in Palestine.

View of the fishermen's harbor at Acre with, out to sea, remains of the so-called Tower of Flies. In the Middle Ages a chain extending from this tower was used to close the harbor. In Jazzar Pasha's time it is said to have been used as a dungeon.

One of the cannons used to defend Acre from attack in the 19th century, still in place on the thick city walls.

The southwestern gate of Acre; the most vulnerable, it was heavily fortified by Jazzar Pasha in the 18th century and by Ibrahim Pasha in the 19th.

View of the walls of Acre with the mosque of Jazzar Pasha on the skyline (left in the picture), and part of the 18th-century walls which withstood the onslaught of Napoleon.

A seal of the Crusader kings of Jerusalem, showing Jean de Brienne, king of Jerusalem in the 13th century.

by the emergence of local leaders who imposed their own rule on whatever territory they could control. Palestine was of little interest to the weak central authorities in Constantinople and the regional rulers were either corrupt or powerless. The end of the 17th century was a renewed period of Messianic turmoil in the Diaspora and greater immigration to the Holy Land. Jews settled in Jerusalem and the community included outstanding scholars who founded synagogues and academies. They once again lived in Hebron, Safed and Tiberias and in the second half of the 18th century, Jews from Poland and Lithuania set up centers of Hassidism in Safed and Tiberias.

Revival of Jewish Settlement

In the second half of the 19th century increased interest by the European powers in the Holy Land brought telegraphic communications, roads, a railway and the resulting economic improvement. The Zionist Movement stimulated new agricultural settlements and the immigration of dedicated pioneers. Development was not only generated from abroad. In 1860 the residents of Jerusalem began to move out of the confines of the city's walls and new neighborhoods were built outside the walls. In 1870 the first agricultural school in the country was founded at Mikveh Israel, and eight years later the Jews of Jerusalem founded the moshava (village) of Petach Tikva.

In 1903 a wave of pogroms in Russia brought about a new wave of immigrants. Between 1904 and 1914 some 40,000 Jews came to Palestine as part of the "Second Aliya." Many returned but those who remained laid the foundations of a new society. In 1909 they established the first kibbutz, or communal settlement, called Degania. They founded a Jewish defense organization *(HaShomer)* to protect the new settlements. They created political parties and, in 1909, began to build

a Jewish suburb on the outskirts of Jaffa, called Tel Aviv. Among them were such leaders as David Ben-Gurion, Itzhak Ben-Zvi and Levi Eshkol.

Members of HaShomer, *one of the self-defense organizations which later formed the Israel Defense Forces.*

The First World War, during which the Turks sided with the Central Powers against the Allies, had a calamitous effect on Palestine. Almost 15% of the Jewish population was forced to leave the country. Large-scale recruitment, heavy taxes and compulsory labor left the remaining population destitute. A locust invasion added to the misery and poverty.

The British Mandate

On December 11, 1917 the British General Edmund Allenby entered Jerusalem. The 400-year Ottoman rule ended and was replaced by British rule, which was to last 30 years. Five years later, the League of Nations confirmed the British Mandate over Palestine.

During the next three decades the desolate land became a thriving country. Moreover, the Jewish community of Palestine developed the infrastructure and institutions of the future Jewish state.

The immigrants of the "Third Aliya" who came from Russia and Poland between 1919 and 1923, were members of Zionist-socialist youth movements. Together with their predecessors they founded the Histradrut — the General Federation of Jewish Labor — and its subsidiaries such as the Solel Boneh (construction company), the Kupat Holim (medical fund), the Tnuva (agricultural marketing cooperative), Bank Hapoalim, Koor Industries and the Hamashbir Department Stores. Numerous new kibbutzim were established, and another type of cooperative settlement, the moshav. The Jezreel Valley was purchased by the Jewish National Fund. Concessions for an electric power plant and the Dead Sea Potash Works were granted to Pinhas

Facsimile of the Balfour Declaration of 2nd November 1917

Sir Herbert Samuel, first High Commissioner of Palestine during the British Mandate period.

(center)
The Balfour Declaration

(right)
Lord Balfour, the British Foreign Secretary.

The Palestine Post headlines during the Arab general strike in 1936.

Rutenberg and Moshe Novomeysky. An Assembly of Deputies and a National Council were elected to deal with Jewish communal affairs.

In 1924 the "Fourth Aliya" began. It consisted mainly of middle-class persons mostly from Poland who invested their funds in building, factories and shops. They contributed to the development of the Jezreel Valley, the Coastal Plain, particularly Tel Aviv, and the Sharon Valley. The Hebrew University was inaugurated in Jerusalem (in 1925) as well as the Haifa Technion. Newspapers and books were published in Hebrew and a Hebrew school system was established.

But British rule also saw increasing violence and enmity between Arabs and Jews in the country. In 1917 the British Foreign Secretary, Lord Balfour, issued his famous declaration stating that the British Government "view with favor the establishment in Palestine of a National Home for the Jewish people." The British, however, had also promised independence to the Arabs and their reign in Palestine was marked by constant efforts to appease the Arabs. Not satisfied by these British efforts, Arab mobs and bands of irregulars attacked Jews in the cities of Jerusalem, Hebron and Safed and isolated Jewish villages. In response, the Jews established the Haganah, a self-defense organization.

During the years 1933 to 1939 the "Fifth Aliya" brought almost 225,000 immigrants into the country legally, and several thousands more who entered illegally. These immigrants, brought large amounts of private capital which were invested in various branches of the economy, particularly construction, industrial enterprises and agriculture. This period, too, saw the establishment of new settlements, especially middle-class settlements, many initiated by recent arrivals from Germany.

In April 1936 the Arab Higher Committee, under the leadership of the nationalist-extremist Mufti of Jerusalem, proclaimed a general strike against the British and demanded the cessation of Jewish immigration into Palestine, the cessation of land purchases by Jews and the formation of a Palestine government. The strike lasted six months and set off a new series of attacks on the Jewish community. The British government appointed the Peel Commission which published its report in 1937 recommending the partition of Palestine into two states — Arab and Jewish. The Jewish leaders accepted the proposal, but the Arabs rejected it and continued their attacks until 1939.

In May 1939 the British government changed its policy in Palestine in an attempt to appease the Arabs in order to keep them from cooper-

The British navy board a ship carrying a load of "illegal" immigrants in Haifa in 1947.

Soldiers of the Jewish Brigade, a British army unit established in 1944, most of whose members were Palestinian Jews.

(right)
Food convoy on its way to Jerusalem, 1948.

Military position in the Old City of Jerusalem, 1948.

ating with the Nazis. A White Paper was issued whereby Jewish immigration was to be restricted to no more than 75,000 over the ensuing five years, and land purchases by Jews were limited to certain sections of the country. The Jews reacted by holding mass demonstrations throughout the country, expanding the illegal immigration activities and establishing new settlements outside the areas permitted by the White Paper.

During the Second World War the Jews cooperated with the British in fighting Hitler but, despite the massacre of European Jewry, the gates of Palestine were kept shut and the few Jews who managed to escape the Nazis entered the country "illegally." Finally, towards the end of the War, the patience of the Jewish community ran out and a variety of underground forces declared a revolt against the British. Exhausted by the struggle against Germany, weary of the bloodletting in Palestine and economically unable to bear the cost of maintaining its troops there, in 1947 Britain turned the Palestine problem over to the newly-formed United Nations. On November 29, 1947 the UN General Assembly voted to partition Palestine into an Arab and a Jewish state.

The Jews announced their acceptance of the United Nations decision but the Arabs proclaimed their determination to go to war to prevent it from being carried out. Violence broke out immediately. With the support of the Arab States, local Arab bands and volunteers from across the borders attacked Jewish settlements and towns. Villages were isolated and Jerusalem was besieged. However, the Jewish underground movements soon organized into an army.

The Palestine Post, *May 16, 1948.*

The State of Israel — The First Years

On May 14, 1948 the last British troops left Palestine and in a moving ceremony David Ben-Gurion read the Declaration of Independence proclaiming the establishment of the State of Israel.

That same evening, the regular armies of the Arab States surrounding Israel invaded the new state. Nevertheless, the Israel Defense Forces (IDF) gradually succeeded in repelling these attacks and by the beginning of 1949, controlled the entire Galilee and the Negev, the Coastal Plain up to Gaza, and the New City of Jerusalem with a corridor connecting it to the rest of the country. The Arabs, on the other hand, had captured the Old City of Jerusalem, with the Jordanian Army holding most of Judea and Samaria (the West Bank of the Jordan River) and the Egyptian Army controlling the Gaza Strip.

Between February and July 1949, Israel signed armistice agreements with Egypt, Jordan and Syria, but these did not lead to peace. Jordan refused to honor its commitment to give the Jews access to their Holy Places in the Old City of Jerusalem; the Syrians continued to harass the settlers in the Galilee who were within range of their guns, and the Egyptians supported terror across the border as a means to continue the war they had lost.

Meanwhile, the Israelis set about building their state. The gates of the country were thrown open to the survivors of the Holocaust and to Jews in communities throughout North Africa and the Middle East. By the end of 1948 more than 100,000 Jews had entered Israel and another 584,000 arrived in the next three years. With the aid of foreign assistance from the United States, contributions from Jews abroad, and a

(left)
Unit of the Palmach on march in the Negev. The Palmach was the voluntary striking force of the Haganah which was incorporated later into the Israel Defense Forces.

Water rationing during the siege of Jerusalem in 1948.

reparations agreement signed with Germany in 1952, the immigrants were absorbed and the economy began to grow. New kibbutzim, villages and towns were established (345 between 1948 and 1951), roads and houses were built, large-scale development projects (such as the draining of the Hula swamps) were begun, the El Al national airline was established, and government corporations were created to exploit Israel's natural resources.

At the same time political institutions were organized. General elections to the country's parliament, the Knesset, gave the Labor Party a plurality. Dr. Chaim Weizmann was elected President of the state and David Ben-Gurion, Prime Minister. Israel was recognized by the United States as well as the Soviet Union and was admitted to the United Nations.

Arab Terrorism and the Sinai Campaign

However, there was still no peace along the borders. Between 1951 and 1956 more than 400 Israelis were killed and 900 wounded by Arab infiltrators and terrorists. The Arabs had instituted a boycott of Israel and blockaded the Gulf of Suez. By 1956 terrorism in the south had become unbearable. A year earlier, Egypt's President Nasser had signed the region's first arms pact with Russia. When Egypt, Syria and Jordan joined in a military pact against Israel, the IDF moved into the Sinai Desert, on October 29, 1956, quickly overrunning Egyptian positions and reaching the shore of the Suez Canal. Britain and France, in an attempt to regain control of the recently nationalized Canal, joined the conflict and bombarded Egyptian positions. The United Nations, led by the United States and Russia, called for a cease-fire and the withdrawal of Egyptian, French and Israeli troops. In March 1957 Israel withdrew after being assured that United Nations troops stationed at Sharm el-Sheikh would keep the sea route to Eilat open, and that UN forces would prevent infiltration from the Gaza Strip.

The new trade route to Asia and Africa opened a gap in the hostile ring which surrounded Israel. New relationships and close ties were established with numerous African and Asian countries to whom Israel supplied technical assistance.

(right)
Egyptian armored unit at Mitla Pass during the Sinai Campaign.

The Israeli ship Bat Galim, *seized by the Egyptians in 1954 at the entrance to the Suez Canal. Its cargo was confiscated and the crew imprisoned.*

Prime Minister David Ben-Gurion inspects the site of the planned road to Sdom.

The Second Decade

In 1958, Israel celebrated its tenth anniversary. Its population had grown to over two million (of whom 940,000 were immigrants), the land under cultivation had increased by 150%, a road had been paved from Beersheba to Eilat, where a port was being built. Industry had doubled its output; unemployment had fallen to 1.4%; half-a-million students attended school.

During the following years the Hadassah organization opened a new Medical Center in Jerusalem and the Israel Museum was completed; Bar-Kochba's letters were discovered in the Judean Desert by Professor Yigael Yadin; an atomic reactor was built at Nahal Sorek; a new port was constructed at Ashdod; the new Knesset building was inaugurated; Shmuel Yosef Agnon received the Nobel Prize for Literature.

On the political scene, Itzhak Ben-Zvi, who had replaced Weizmann as President, died and was succeeded by Zalman Shazar; David Ben-Gurion resigned as Prime Minister and was replaced by Levi Eshkol; Israel and West Germany agreed to establish diplomatic relations.

The Third Decade — From War to Peace

The relatively peaceful ten years ended in May 1967 when Egypt moved troops into Sinai and Nasser ordered the United Nations forces

First Independence Day Parade.

Egyptian aircraft destroyed on the ground at the beginning of the Six Day War.

Israeli troops at Sharm el-Sheikh.

Israeli armor on the Golan Heights, 1967.

out of Sharm el-Sheikh, reimposing the blockage of the Gulf of Suez. As the nations of the world stood helpless in the face of this blatant disregard of international guarantees and Israel's friends were gripped with fear for its safety, Israel, on June 5, executed a pre-emptive air strike which destroyed Arab air power on the ground. During the next six days, the IDF routed the Egyptians, capturing the Gaza Strip and Sinai and once again reaching the banks of the Suez Canal. In the north, the Syrians were driven off the Golan Heights after a bitter battle. When Jordan rebuffed Israel's pleas to remain out of the war and attacked, Israeli forces took all the land up to the Jordan River, recapturing the Old City and the Western Wall in Jerusalem, the Etzion Bloc, Hebron and Jericho. Jerusalem, which had been unnaturally divided for nineteen years, was once again reunified.

In the wake of the Six Day War, Israel has established settlements throughout the West Bank (also known as Judea and Samaria), and annexed the Old City of Jerusalem. But it has established an "open bridges" policy allowing free movement of persons and goods over the border with Jordan, permitted the organization of local colleges and universities, authorized the publication of newspapers and journals,

Defense Minister Moshe Dayan, center, Commander in Chief Yizhak Rabin, right, and Commander of the Central Area Forces Uzi Narkiss enter the Old City of Jerusalem through St. Stephen's Gate, June 7, 1967.

Aerial view of the 1968 Independence Day Parade.

allowed employment throughout Israel, improved the infrastructure, held local elections and generally raised the standard of living in the territories — all of which were never done by Jordan during its 19-year rule of the West Bank. Moreover, despite the division in Israeli public opinion regarding the future of the territories, Israel has never closed the door to territorial concessions in return for peace.

In September 1968 Egypt began massive artillery attacks across the cease-fire lines. The fighting escalated into the War of Attrition with Egyptian bombardments and Israeli air raids deep into Egypt coming to an end in August 1970 with an American initiated cease-fire.

Terrorist attacks, highlighted by the hijacking of civilian aircraft, also resumed. In 1972 eleven Israeli athletes were murdered at the Olympic Games in Munich and a group of terrorists machine-gunned 27 pilgrims to death at Ben-Gurion Airport. In 1974, 24 school children were murdered by terrorists in northern Israel.

Prime Minister Levi Eshkol died in 1969 and was succeeded by Golda Meir. Immigration increased beginning in 1970, with an influx of newcomers from both the Western countries and the Soviet Union. The economy revived and the standard of living rose.

Shmuel Yosef Agnon receives the Nobel Prize for Literature in Stockholm in 1966. King Gustav VI, on the left, applauds him.

French-built gunboats brought to Israel from Cherbourg in 1969 in defiance of a French arms embargo.

Prime Minister Golda Meir and Defense Minister Moshe Dayan with the troops on the Golan Heights during the Yom Kippur War.

(right)
Syrian tanks on the Golan Heights.

On October 6, 1973, on Yom Kippur — Judaism's holiest day, Egypt and Syria launched a two-front attack on Israel. Taking Israel by surprise, the Egyptians quickly crossed the Suez Canal and the Syrian forces overran the Golan Heights. But the Israeli forces recovered, repulsed the attacking forces until they had surrounded the Egyptian Third Army on the west bank of the Suez Canal and recaptured the Golan, coming to a halt some 20 miles from Damascus.

Following the cease-fire (on October 24), Israel and Egypt negotiated an agreement under the auspices of U.S. Secretary of State Henry Kissinger for the exchange of prisoners and the release of the beleaguered Third Army. In January 1974 the two countries signed a separation of forces agreement, and a similar agreement was brought about between Syria and Israel in May 1974. In September 1975 Egypt and Israel signed an additional agreement under which Israel withdrew even further from the Suez Canal, giving up strategic passes in the Sinai and the Abu Rodeis oilfields.

Despite the demoralizing effect of the Yom Kippur War, the ruling Labor Party won a renewed mandate in December 1973. The following year, however, Prime Minister Golda Meir resigned and was replaced by Yitzhak Rabin. In 1975 the Suez Canal was reopened and an Israeli-

Danny Kaye visits the troops during the Yom Kippur War.

U.S. Secretary of State Henry Kissinger, who played a major role in the negotiations between Israel and the Arab states after the Yom Kippur War, meeting Prime Minister Golda Meir in 1974.

bound cargo passed through it. 100,000 immigrants from the Soviet Union arrived in the country. A trade agreement was signed between Israel and the European Economic Community. Prices continued to rise and successive devaluations lowered the value of the Israeli currency.

Terrorist attacks continued and, in 1976, Israeli troops staged a dramatic rescue of over 100 hostages held by terrorist hijackers at Uganda's Entebbe Airport. That same year, the "Good Fence" was opened on the Israel–Lebanon border, allowing victims of the civil war between Muslims and Christians to seek medical aid in Israel.

In December 1976 the Rabin Government resigned and new parliamentary elections were set for May 1977. On that date, the Israeli public, unexpectedly, for the first time, swept the Labor Party from office. Menachem Begin, heading a Likud Party coalition, was elected Prime Minister.

Hostages held by terrorist hijackers at Entebbe Airport in 1976 return home after their dramatic rescue by Israeli troops.

The Fourth Decade of Statehood

Begin, as had each Prime Minister before him, extended an invitation to the heads of the surrounding Arab States to meet with him and conduct direct negotiations towards signing a peace treaty without prior conditions. To the surprise of the world (but after much secret preparation), Egyptian President Anwar Sadat accepted the invitation and, in November 1977, came to Jerusalem to meet Israeli leaders and address the Knesset.

Egyptian President Anwar Sadat on arrival at Ben-Gurion Airport in November 1977. On the left is Prime Minister Menachem Begin.

During his visit to the Knesset, President Sadat listens through earphones to a simultaneous translation of the speech of Prime Minister Menachem Begin, on the left.

Sixteen months later, on March 26, 1979, Israel and Egypt formally signed a peace treaty on the lawn of the White House in Washington. The negotiating process was long and involved. It required the personal involvement of U.S. President Jimmy Carter and a dramatic summit meeting at Camp David to reach a successful conclusion. Egypt, on the one hand, broke the Arab consensus against direct negotiations with

Israel and, as a result, was almost totally isolated within the Arab world. Israel, on the other hand, conceded all of Sinai with its strategic depth, vital oil and air fields, and Israeli settlements. However, the thirty-year long state of war between the two countries has been ended and both Sadat and Begin received the Nobel Peace Prize for their accomplishment.

Further progress was nevertheless stalled. Talks between Israel and Egypt, leading to full autonomy for Palestine Arabs in Judea, Samaria

President Sadat, left, U.S. President Jimmy Carter, center, and Prime Minister Begin signing the peace treaty.

Menachem Begin receives the Nobel Peace Prize.

and the Gaza Strip, as agreed in the Camp David accord for a framework for peace in the Middle East, broke down in September 1980 when it became apparent that Egyptian and Israeli interpretations were vastly different. A year later, in October 1981, Sadat was assassinated by Moslem extremists.

In Israel, Begin won a second election in June 1981, and appointed

The Likud headquarters on receipt of the news of its success in the 1981 elections to the Knesset.

Ariel Sharon as Minister of Defense. The Begin Government's policy of supporting the Christians in the civil war in Lebanon, in order to contain the terrorists entrenched there, had led, in March 1978, to the occupation by Israel of a ten-mile strip north of the border, in retaliation for a terrorist attack in Israel in which a large number of Israeli citizens were killed. The strengthening of the terrorists' position after Israel withdrew, and renewed attacks on Israeli towns in the north, led to Operation Peace for the Galilee in June 1982.

Israeli troops destroyed the PLO terrorists' infrastructure in Lebanon and forced them to retreat from Beirut. However, the assassination of the Christian President, Bashir Jemayel, the massacre of Palestinians by the Christian forces in the Sabra and Shatilla refugee camps, and increased local opposition to the Israeli presence, strengthened the position of the Israelis opposed to the war.

In September 1983 Menachem Begin resigned as Prime Minister.

Israeli soldiers distribute candy to children during the war in Lebanon.

The people
of Israel

Who are the Israelis? Where do they come from? Where and how do they live? The following facts and figures sketch a portrait of a diverse, heterogeneous, yet united people, who have created a new life in their ancient homeland.

In the 1st century CE it is estimated that some three million people lived in the Holy Land. War and conquest, brigandage and plunder, exile and slavery, natural disasters and poverty all combined to reduce this number to less than 200,000 in the 16th century. Three hundred years later there were less than 300,000 in the country and about 500,000 at the beginning of the 20th century. Today, some 4,400,000 persons live in the State of Israel, including about 50,000 Israeli residents living in Judea, Samaria and the Gaza Strip. In addition, the population of the areas administered by Israel numbers more than 1.3 million.

Young Sabras — native-born Israelis — and the prickly pear plants whose sweet fruit, protected by a thorny exterior, gave them their nickname.

At the end of 1987, the Jewish community numbered 3.6 million Jews, an increase from 24,000 persons in 1882 by 150-fold in a little more than one hundred years. The main factor behind this increase was *aliya* — immigration or return to the Land of Israel, which was and remains the essence of the Zionist Movement and the Jewish State which it created. More than 2.3 million Jews came to Israel in the past 105 years, three-quarters of them — 1.8 million — after the State of Israel was created in 1948 and threw open its doors to Jews throughout the world who sought refuge from oppression or desired to be part of the Jewish renaissance.

At first, the waves of immigration were numbered. The First Aliya, from 1882 to 1903, brought 25,000 Jews, doubling the existing Jewish community in the country. The Second Aliya (1904–1914), which laid the foundations of the country's economic and social fabric, brought 40,000. The Third Aliya (1918–1922) included 35,000 immigrants, and the Fourth, 90,000 persons between 1923 and 1932. With the rise of the Nazi Party in Germany, the pace of those seeking refuge increased. During the Fifth Aliya (1933–1939) about 225,000 Jews from Germany, Eastern Europe and Central Europe immigrated to Palestine. Another 130,000 refugees managed to enter the country between 1939 and 1948, despite the barriers erected by the British.

During the first three and a half years of statehood, from May 15, 1948 until the end of 1951, almost all the survivors of the Nazi Holocaust, as well as entire communities from the Middle East and North Africa, immigrated to Israel. The 680,000 persons who came during those years again doubled the existing Jewish community in the coun-

Children celebrating Independence Day.

try. In the thirty-five years beginning in 1952 nearly 1.1 million more Jews have come to live in Israel.

The majority of Jews living in Israel today, almost 60%, were born in the country. Moreover, more than 19% of the Jewish population are second generation Israelis, born to parents who were also born in the country.

The remainder of the Jews of Israel, just over 40% of the total, were born in Europe and the Americas (21%), in Africa (almost 10%) and in Asia (8%). The Asian and African Jews came from such countries as Aden, Algeria, Egypt, Ethiopia, India, Iran, Iraq, Libya, Morocco, Tunisia, Turkey and Yemen. The Europeans immigrated from East Europe (Russia, Poland, Latvia, Lithuania, Bulgaria and Romania), Central Europe (Austria, Czechoslovakia, Germany and Hungary), and other countries such as Belgium, Britain, France, Greece, Holland and Italy. The Americans included Jews from the United States, Canada, Central America and Latin America.

Israelis, on the whole, are young. Almost half the population (49%) is under 25 years old, with 30% below 15. More than a quarter of the population is between the ages of 25 and 44, 15% between 45 and 64 and 9% 65 and over. Those born in Israel constitute the bulk of the age group below 20 (over 1.2 million), while less than 200,000 are over 40. Those born abroad, on the other hand, are mainly in the older age group with more than 800,000 aged 45 and 64, of the total of nearly 1.2 million over age 30.

More Israelis live in the Tel Aviv District (almost 24%), than anywhere else in the country. This area, combined with the surrounding Central District, contains almost half (45%) of Israel's total population. More than 16% live in the Galilee's Northern District and almost 14% in the Haifa District. The remaining 25% are almost evenly divided between the Jerusalem District in the middle of the country, and the Southern District, which includes the Negev.

This distribution of the population is largely a result of the Israeli's affinity for urban life. Nearly 90% of the people live in urban locations, of which one quarter are to be found in the three large cities of Jerusa-

Well-planned and integrated housing development in the neighborhood of Haifa.

lem, Tel Aviv and Haifa. There are a total of 92 such localities throughout the country, ranging in size from a population of 2,000 to over 200,000.

Of the 10% of Israelis who live in one of the more than 900 rural localities, 6.5% live in the unique Israeli collectives known as *kibbutzim* (268) and *moshavim* (458).

Experiments in Living

The kibbutz, a combined product of Zionism, socialism and Judaism, was one of the first experiments by the Jewish pioneers to change the character of both the people and the land. The first kibbutz was Degania, established on the southern shore of the Sea of Galilee in 1909 by a group of pioneers of the Second Aliya who were imbued by the concept of social justice, convinced that physical labor was the highest human value, and dedicated to the importance of identifying with nature and the Land. It was funded by the Zionist Organization's Palestine Office and settled on land purchased by the Jewish National Fund. By 1914, 11 kibbutzim had been established and by the end of 1918 there were 29.

The scientific approach to agriculture involves constant monitoring of the crop's progress.

(central picture)
Performance by a Jewish-Arab
folk dance group.
The surrounding pictures show
some of the many faces of the
people of Israel.

Yemenite family celebrating the Passover seder *service.*

Torah scribe at work.

A few years after the establishment of the first kibbutz, a number of pioneers sought a form of settlement that would provide more freedom for individual initiative and farm management while still applying some of the collective principles of the kibbutz. Thus, in 1921 the first *moshav*, Nahalal, was founded in the Jezreel Valley.

The moshav is a cooperative smallholders' village with each family owning its own home and farm. The cooperative owns the heavy machinery, erects all public buildings, markets the produce and purchases supplies collectively. It provides local or regional education, medical care and cultural services. Some moshavim also engage in industry, and major packing houses and plants are maintained by a number of regional moshav consortiums. The management of the moshav is democratically elected by its members.

In 1936 the first *moshav shitufi* was founded, in an attempt to find the "golden mean" between what its members considered the over-collectivism of the kibbutz and the over-emphasis on individual farming of the moshav. Thus, in the moshav shitufi the lands and buildings are owned collectively, but each family has its own home, raises its own children and is provided with funds to meet its needs. Education, medical services and cultural activities are provided collectively.

Most of the newcomers who came to Israel shortly after the State was declared had little interest in kibbutz life. However, the family-based moshav movement provided an excellent opportunity for the settlement of large numbers of families and even entire communities in unsettled areas. Thus, during the period between 1949 and 1956 some 250 new moshavim were established. The need to provide adequate services to these and other often isolated communities led to the development of the "rural cluster," or Lachish Plan, which links several villages to a local rural center and a number of centers to a regional town.

The Hebrew Language

As unique as the social experiment in collective living was Israel's revolution in reviving the ancient Hebrew language, transforming it into the daily tongue of an entire nation, making it the vehicle of outstanding literature, and influencing thousands of Jews outside of Israel to study and use it.

From biblical times until the Babylonian exile, the language of the People of Israel was Hebrew. In Babylon the Jews learned Aramaic and brought it back with them to the Holy Land. Hebrew, however, remained the spoken language of the Jews until the end of the Second Temple period in the 1st century. Exiled from the Land of Israel the Jews throughout the Diaspora learned and used a wide variety of other languages. Hebrew remained the language of prayer and study, of the Bible, the Law and the Holy Books, uniting the people despite their dispersion. But this and the various revivals of the language over the centuries, was a far cry from the daily language of a people and a country.

Then, in 1881, Eliezer Ben-Yehuda arrived in Palestine. Devoted to the Zionist cause, Ben-Yehuda insisted that the people could only be united if they revived their ancient language. He spoke Hebrew exclusively and in 1883 secured permission to use it in his post as teacher at the Alliance Israélite Universelle school in Jerusalem. Soon other teachers joined him, devising terminologies and textbooks in mathematics, geography and other subjects. In 1888 the local school in Rishon LeZion became the first to teach all its courses in Hebrew. Ben-Yehuda formed the Hebrew Language Academy which fixed spelling and grammar rules and devised new words. He also compiled material

A rabbi deep in study.

Members of the ancient Samaritan sect, an offshoot of Judaism dating from the 8th century BCE, celebrate Passover at their holy site on Mount Gerizim outside Nablus.

Non-Jewish Citizens of Israel

Non-Jews comprise almost 18% of the Israeli population, some 800,000 persons. Three-quarters of these are Muslim Arabs, almost 13% are Christians — mostly Arab — and the remaining 9.5% are Druze, Circassians, Karaites and Samaritans.

The majority of Israeli non-Jews live in the Northern and Haifa Districts (63%), with an additional 18% residing in Jerusalem and its surrounding villages. The Muslims and Druze have one of the highest birthrates in the world, leading to a rate of natural increase of 32.3 (as compared to 17.1 for the Jews). As a result they are very young, with the median age of the Muslims just under 16 (as compared to over 27 for the Jews), and three-quarters of the non-Jews in Israel are below the age of 30. The life expectancy of the Israeli Arab has risen from 52 years in 1948 to 71.5 years today.

Armenian religious procession starting from the Church of the Holy Sepulcher.

Ethiopian Christians in Jerusalem. The Ethiopian community claims its religious center was established in Jerusalem from about the 8th century.

Israeli Arabs enjoy full equality before the law and Arabic is the State's official second language. There is a network of Arab schools throughout the country and compulsory education is applicable, as in the Jewish community, through twelfth grade. Both Arabs and Druze are represented in the Knesset and serve as deputy ministers and in senior government posts. There are 60 local Arab councils and additional villages are represented on regional councils.

Arab woman voting in the Knesset elections.

A resident of the Old City of Jerusalem.

Israeli law has changed the status of Arab women by providing full voting rights, prohibiting bigamy, child marriage and divorce without the consent of the wife, and instituting free and compulsory primary education for girls. An increasing number of girls complete high school, with some continuing their education at professional schools and universities, and a growing number of women are employed outside the home.

The impact of Israeli society has weakened the often autocratic authority of village elders and the heads of families and has led to an increasingly powerful, active and educated younger generation. Bedouin tribes in both the north and south are gradually being settled in permanent housing.

Since the non-Jewish population is culturally and nationally Arab, as are the surrounding countries, Israeli Arabs are not required to serve in the Israel Defense Forces. Nevertheless, numerous Bedouin have volunteered for military service. Druze and Circassians, at their request, have been subject to conscription since the late 1950s, with the same terms of service as apply to Jews.

In the past forty years, the people of Israel, Jews and non-Jews alike, have grown into a united nation. Differences still exist, as do gaps in educational and economic levels, but the will and the effort are being made to make the society a truly egalitarian one.

Religious life

For millions of people throughout the world, the Holy Land is the cradle of civilization, the birthplace and spiritual center of three monotheistic religions — Judaism, Christianity and Islam. To the Jews it is the Promised Land and the Land of Israel. To the Christians, it is the source of their faith, the place where Jesus was born, where he preached, and where he died on the cross. To the Muslims, it is the site of the holy shrines, the Mosque of El Aksa and the Dome of the Rock. To the people of all religions, it is a country filled with history and significance, a place where holy sites abound, the Land of the Bible, a home for the devout, and a magnet for pilgrims.

The fact that the country is the focus of religious belief, worship and even fanaticism has, in the past, led to strife and warfare. Today, on the other hand, the State of Israel guarantees freedom of religion, scrupulously safeguards the inviolability of the Holy Places of all faiths, and allows each denomination the right to maintain its own religious and charitable institutions and to administer its internal affairs.

Under Islamic rule, religious beliefs and adherence took on a peculiar and significant communal character. Since Islam does not distinguish between "church" and "state," with the latter exercising both functions, the ruling Muslims had no need to organize religiously. However, non-Muslims required an organization recognized by the government, in order to protect their rights and interests. As a result, the Ottoman rulers recognized a number of Christian communities, known as "millets." These communities were corporate entities of semi-national characterstics and internal autonomy, especially in matters of personal status such as marriage, divorce and inheritance, which were under the jurisdiction of their religious courts.

The millet system was maintained by the British under the Mandate for Palestine, but modified to the extent that it also recognized the Jewish and Muslim communities. In general terms, the system was also adopted and legally recognized by the State of Israel. The religious courts of each community still have jurisdiction over certain matters of personal status; religious designation still carries a national connotation, and the internal affairs of each community, including religious education, are run by members of that faith, largely autonomously.

Thus, despite the fact that Israel is a Jewish state, there is no state religion, and all religions are treated equally. While the Jewish Sabbath and Jewish festivals are national holidays, each community has the statutory right to observe its own day of rest and its holy days. The Ministry of Religious Affairs cooperates closely with each religious group. It supervises the Holy Places, supports theological seminaries, subsidizes the construction of synagogues, churches and mosques, and audits and financially assists the religious councils which every local authority is required to appoint by law.

Pentateuch scroll case, decorated with silver-gilt designs on wood, from Baghdad, Iraq, 1852. The twin glass plates on the inside of the cupola are inscribed with biblical passages.

The Jewish Community

The Chief Rabbinate is recognized by Israeli law as the supreme religious authority for the country's Jews.

Under the Turks, the supreme religious and judicial authority of the Jews was the Hakham Bashi, or Chief Rabbi of the Sephardim. The imperial appointment was made in 1841, a few months after the Sultan issued a *firman* (decree) protecting the rights of the Jews, and it is from this year that the formal organization of the Jewish religious community in the country in modern times can be dated.

During the next half century or so, the Ashkenazi community in the country, particularly in Jerusalem, grew larger and stronger, eventually replacing the Sephardim as the dominant community. With the end of Turkish rule the office of Hakham Bashi ceased to exist, while the office of president of the Ashkenazi religious courts had remained unfilled for a number of years. In 1920, the British appointed a commission to study the creation of a united Chief Rabbinate for the entire country. A year later, a group of 21 electors chose Rabbi Abraham Isaac Kook and Rabbi Ya'akov Meir as the first Ashkenazi and Sephardi Chief Rabbis.

The two rabbis headed the Chief Rabbinate Council which was recognized by the government as the supreme religious body of the Jews. In 1953 the Knesset legally confirmed this arrangement. However, from its inception until today, the ultra-Orthodox Jews of the country refuse to recognize the Chief Rabbi's authority, insisting upon choosing their own rabbis and religious courts.

The rabbinate and the religious courts have jurisdiction over all mat-

Miniature from the 15th century Darmstadt Haggadah, *showing a Jewish family celebrating the* Passover *seder service.* *(Darmstadt Landesbibliothek)*

The traditional tomb of King David on Mount Zion. Since the Middle Ages it has been a focus of Jewish pilgrimage.

rimonial cases involving Jewish residents of the country, including marriage, divorce, and child support. The Chief Rabbinical Council has departments for the supervision of dietary laws, the regulation of scribes, the approval of registrars of marriages, the sanction of rabbinical ordination, and the issuing of responsa in matters of religious law.

The two Chief Rabbis preside over the Supreme Rabbinical Court which hears appeals from the 12 rabbinical courts. Local religious needs and services are provided by some 200 regional councils, which are financed jointly by the State and the local authorities. The councils are under the religious authority of the Chief Rabbinate and are administered by the Ministry of Religious Affairs. There are some 7,000 synagogues throughout the country and about 500 appointed rabbis.

A Bar Mitzva *ceremony at Masada.*

Booths in the courtyard of the Orthodox Jewish quarter of Mea She'arim in Jerusalem during the festival of Succot (the Feast of Tabernacles). Booths covered with branches of myrtle and other trees are erected in courtyards and gardens, and even on balconies during the festival.

Jewish education is provided by the state religious schools, which teach both religious and secular studies, by an independent educational network which is more religious than the state system but recognized and supervised by the State, and by a variety of *yeshivot*. The more than 600 yeshivot throughout the country emphasize intensive religious study, catering to male and female students of all ages.

Although the Jewish Sabbath and festivals are national holidays, with almost all stores, offices, restaurants and factories closed, no newspapers published, and most public transportation suspended, there is still a great deal of activity on these days. Radio and television broadcast, private cars and taxis fill the roads, sports matches are held, and thousands of Israelis spend the holidays on the country's beaches

The festival of Succot (or the Feast of Tabernacles) celebrated at the Western Wall in Jerusalem.

*Interior of the synagogue at
Yemin Moshe, Jerusalem.*

*Tomb of Maimonides, the great-
est medieval Jewish scholar, physician and philosopher, near
Tiberias.*

Tomb believed to be that of Moses Hayyim Luzzatto known also as Ramhal, the famous Italian 18th-century kabbalist, writer of ethical works and Hebrew poetry, near Tiberias.

Tomb at Tiberias of Rabbi Meir Ba'al Ha-Ness, one of the great Tannaim, the 2nd-century rabbis who were the fathers of the Talmud.

and in its parks. Such public services as telephones, electricity, and water pumps continue to function on the Sabbath. Jewish dietary laws are observed throughout the army and in all government and public institutions and the religious needs of Israeli soldiers are supplied by the Chaplaincy.

Non-Orthodox Jewish congregations, such as the Reform and Conservative, have increased their activities in Israel in recent years, however, neither they nor their rabbis are recognized by the Chief Rabbinate and they are not permitted to perform weddings, grant divorces or carry out conversions.

Over the years, a number of religious controversies have gripped the country. These have ranged from the exemption of yeshiva students from army service to the question of "Who is a Jew" (religious law insists that the mother be Jewish or that an Orthodox conversion take place). Generally a modus vivendi has been reached which is broken only in isolated cases.

The Six Day War in 1967 resulted in Jews once again being permitted to pray at some of their most venerated Holy Places, from which they had been barred for nineteen years, including the Western Wall in Jerusalem, Rachel's Tomb just outside of Bethlehem, and the Tomb of the Patriarchs in Hebron. These and such other tombs as those of Maimonides, Rabbi Shimon Bar Yochai and Rabbi Meir Ba'al Haness in the Galilee, as well as King David's Tomb in Jerusalem, are some of the places in the country related to religious observance and feelings.

The "breastplate" or shield hanging from the staves of a scroll of the Law recalls the breastplate worn by the High Priest. The one shown here is from Munich, 1826. (Israel Museum)

A **Hanukia,** *or Hanukah lamp, lit on each evening of the eight-day Festival of Lights which commemorates the victory of the Maccabees over the Hellenistic armies in 164 BCE.*

Devout Jew praying at the Western Wall in Jerusalem.

The Christian Communities

There were some 100,000 Christians living in Israel at the end of 1987, most of whom were Arabs, belonging to some thirty different denominations.

The Greek Orthodox is the oldest ecclesiastical body in the Holy Land, dating back to 451 CE. It prospered in Byzantine times but was superseded by a Latin Patriarch during the Crusades. Under the Ottoman Turks the Greek Orthodox stood at the head of the Christian millet but their position was threatened by the Latins, who were protected by France. The two rival groups strove to secure primacy over Christian Holy Places in the Holy Land, first one then the other gaining the upper hand, often with the aid of European allies and "protectors." Finally, in 1852 Sultan Abdul Mejid issued a *firman* determining the "status quo" of the rights of the various churches to the Holy Places, based on the situation which existed in 1757 which favored the Greek Orthodox. This status quo was reaffirmed a number of times by the Turks and the British, and was given binding status by the State of Israel.

The recognized Christian communities in Israel include the Eastern

The Chapel of the Angel, the antechamber to the tomb of Jesus, in the Church of the Holy Sepulcher in Jerusalem.

(Greek) Orthodox, the Roman Catholics (or Latins), the Gregorian and the Catholic Armenians, the Syrian Catholics, the Uniate Chaldeans, the Greek Catholic or Melkites, the Maronites, the Syrian Orthodox, the Copts and the Ethiopians. The Church of England and the Evangelical Lutheran Church were subsequently recognized by Jordan and in 1970 Israel recognized the Evangelical Episcopal Church.

The headquarters of the Christian religious communities are located in Jerusalem which is the seat of three Patriarchates, the Greek Orthodox, the Latin and the Armenian Orthodox. The Anglican, Greek Catholic, Coptic, Syrian and Ethiopian Archbishops and Bishops also reside in the Holy City, which is the site of the venerated Church of the Holy Sepulcher, containing the Tomb of Jesus. The Church is administered mainly by the Greek Orthodox, Latins and Armenians, with the Syrians and Copts controlling small chapels within the Church, and the Ethiopians and Anglicans using nearby chapels. The Sepulcher of the Virgin Mary and the Church of Ascension on the Mount of Olives, as well as the Church and Grotto of the Nativity in Bethlehem, are also administered jointly by the various Christian communities under the status quo agreement.

Courtyard of the Church of the Visitation, Ein Karem, where the words of Mary rejoicing that she was to be the mother of Jesus, known as the Magnificat, are inscribed on ceramic plaques in forty-two languages.

A star in the Grotto of the Nativity in Bethlehem marks the spot where Jesus is said to have been born. Seventeen lamps burn perpetually above the star.

The Greek Orthodox Church is headed by the Patriarch of Jerusalem with jurisdiction over the entire Holy Land. The Patriarchate owns some 45 monasteries and numerous churches throughout the country. Its seat in Jerusalem is the Convent of Constantine (once a Crusader palace) with a magnificent library of thousands of ancient manuscripts.

Of the two Russian Orthodox Churches, also seated in Jerusalem, one represents the Russian Patriarchate of Moscow, and the other is part of the Russian Church in Exile, centered in New York.

The Latin Patriarchate has jurisdiction over all Roman Catholics in the Holy Land, Jordan and Cyprus. The largest and most important of the some 40 Latin religious orders and communities are the Franciscans, who established a monastery on Mt. Zion in 1334 and who are the custodians of the major Catholic sanctuaries in the country. While their part of the Church of the Holy Sepulcher is the most important Catholic site, there are some 70 other churches and chapels under their

Greek Orthodox monastery at Capernaum, an ancient village on the shore of the Sea of Galilee where Jesus preached.

RELIGIOUS LIFE

control throughout the country. The community also administers some
40 schools and kindergartens, five hospitals, 4 clinics and 13 hospices
for pilgrims.

The Greek Catholics or Melkites are among the largest Catholic communities in the country. They have more than 30 places of worship, as
well as numerous schools, seminaries, orphanages and clinics.

All the Patriarchs of the Uniate Churches (the Oriental churches in
communion with Rome), including the Maronite, Chaldean, and Syrian and Armenian Catholic, reside in Arab countries, but their jurisdiction is recognized in Israel and they are represented by vicars in
Jerusalem. They do not have rights in the principal Holy Places.

The Armenian Church is the largest of the Monophysitic or non-
Chalcedonian Churches, and its Patriarch is equal in rank to the Greek
Orthodox and Latin Patriarchs, with whom he shares the basilicas of
the Church of the Holy Sepulcher and the Church of the Nativity. The
Cathedral and Convent of the Church are located in the Armenian
Quarter of the Old City of Jerusalem, in a compound which also houses
a valuable library, historic treasures, a printing press and a seminary,
forming the largest monastic center in Israel.

The Anglican and Protestant Churches first came to the Holy Land
at the beginning of the 19th century, with the Protestants initially con-
centrating on missionary work among the Jews. Among the Protestant
groups in the country are the Anglican Church (Church of England),
the Lutheran Church, the Baptist Church, the Church of Scotland, the
Church of the Nazarene, the Pentecostal Movement, the Adventist
Church, the Church of Christ, the Society of Friends (Quakers), the
Seventh Day Adventists and the Jehovah's Witnesses. Recognized by
the Israel Government as a community on April 12, 1970, they are the
smallest of all Israel's Christian groups.

The annual procession which marks the beginning of the Holy Week for the Latin Church in Jerusalem. It enters the Old City through St. Stephen's Gate.

The Muslim Community

With the establishment of the State of Israel, Muslim public life collapsed because of the flight of almost all Arab leaders, including religious authorities. Through the Ministry of Religious Affairs, Israel gradually rebuilt the institutions of the Muslim community. Six local "*sharia*" (religious) courts were established in Acre, Beersheba, Haifa, Jaffa, Nazareth and Tayyiba with jurisdiction over the personal status of Muslims. Muslim trusteeship committees were etablished to attend to the community's religious and social affairs, to administer the revenues of the *waqf* (endowment) properties, and to manage the Muslim Holy Places. The Ministry of Religious Affairs helps maintain some 135 mosques throughout the country, as well as more than 200 Muslim cemeteries, and pays the salaries of nearly 300 religious judges (Qadis) and other functionaries.

Interior of El Aksa Mosque. Originally built in the 8th century, it was destroyed by earthquakes and its present form dates to the 11th century.

Fridays and Islamic religious holy days are officially recognized holidays for Muslims. The Arabic station of the Israel Broadcasting Authority airs daily readings from the Koran, as well as prayers and sermons from the principal mosques on Fridays and holidays. Religion is taught in the primary and post-primary schools of the Arab educational system.

The reunification of Jerusalem in 1967 enabled all Israeli Muslims to pray at the El Aksa Mosque, the third in importance in the Islamic world, for the first time since 1948. Israel has left the *sharia* courts of Jerusalem, Judea and Samaria and the Gaza Strip undisturbed, and has provided facilities for the Muslims of these areas, as well as Israeli Muslims, to fulfill the fifth pillar of the Islamic faith, the pilgrimage to Mecca.

Other Religious Groups

The Druze sect, of which there are about 70,000 members in Israel, originated in the 11th century, when it broke away from Islam. Despite the fact that they speak Arabic and that their cultural and social patterns are similar to those of other Arabs, the Druze have maintained their separate existence by a strict prohibition against intermarriage and a strong sense of communal solidarity.

During the 1948 War of Independence, the Druze opted to join the Jewish forces against the Arabs. They served as volunteers in the Israeli Army until 1957 when they became part of the regular compulsory draft system, and when they were granted the status of an autonomous religious community.

Interior of the Mosque of Jazzar Pasha in Acre, built at the end of the 18th century.

Interior of a Druze shrine assumed to be the burial place of Jethro, with whom Nebi Shueib, the leading prophet of the sect, is identified.

The Druze live in villages on the Carmel Mountain range, in the Galilee and on the Golan Heights. There is an annual Druze pilgrimage to the Tomb of Jethro, the father-in-law of Moses, whom they venerate.

About 5,000 Circassians live in two villages in the Galilee. They are Sunni Muslims from the Caucasus, who have become well integrated into Israeli life and serve in the Israeli Army.

The spiritual and administrative center of the world religion known as Baha'ism is located at the Bahai Temple in Haifa, which houses the tomb of the movement's founder, the Bab. The tomb of Baha'ullah, near Acre, is considered the holiest of the Bahai shrines.

Exterior of the Druze shrine of Nebi Shueib at the foot of the Horns of Hittin in Galilee.

More than 15,000 Karaites live in Israel today. They are members of a Jewish sect which has rejected rabbinical law and adheres strictly to the Five Books of Moses. Although not regarded as a separate community, they have their own religious courts.

The ancient sect of Samaritans also only recognize the authority of the Pentateuch. Numbering just over 500, they live in Holon and Nablus and they consider nearby Mount Gerizim, where they celebrate their Passover sacrifice, as the true site of the Temple.

Thus the Holy Land remains a kaleidoscope of faiths and religions, each free to practice its own beliefs, supervise its own affairs, and control its own places of worship which are protected by law.

The Bahai temple on Mount Carmel, Haifa.

(top left)
The library at the Bahai complex on Mount Carmel.

(bottom left)
Nablus, the biblical Shechem, the center of the Samaritan sect.

A Samaritan priest displays a Torah scroll.

Zionism
Return to the Land

The concept of "returning to Zion," or Zionism, began when the Jews were first sent into exile in 586 BCE, but continued to dream of their homeland. As the Psalmist wrote: "By the rivers of Babylon we sat and wept when we remembered Zion."

The first expression of Zionism was religious and early rabbinical statements praised those who lived in the Holy Land. With the destruction of the Second Temple and the arrangement of the daily prayers, the longing for Zion, Israel and Jerusalem became even more explicit. Three times a day Jews prayed "to gather our exiles . . . from the four corners of the earth." They insisted: "If I forget thee, O Jerusalem, let my right hand wither."

It is not surprising, therefore, that the return to the Holy Land was a key concept of the Jewish messianic movements. It was the Messiah who would redeem the People of Israel and restore them to their Land, and the numerous pseudo-messiahs who arose throughout Jewish history proclaimed an end to the exile.

Beginning in the 16th century, numerous non-Jews advocated the establishment of a Jewish state in the Holy Land. A Restoration Movement of mainly pietistic Protestants was founded in England by Thomas Brightman. In 1695 Holger Pauli, a Danish merchant, proposed elaborate schemes for the establishment of a Jewish monarchy in Palestine. Twenty years later, the Marquis de Langallerie began negotiations with the Turkish Ambassador at The Hague for a homeland for the Jews. In 1799 Napoleon called on the Jews, as "the rightful heirs of Palestine," to claim "political existence as a nation."

The Israeli flag carried by Gadna youth during a parade in Jerusalem. The flag of the State, two blue stripes on a white background with the "Shield of David" in the center, originally the banner of the Zionist movement, was first displayed in 1891 by the Boston Benei Zion Society. It was adopted as the national flag six months after Israel's proclamation of independence.

The 19th century saw the development of wide-ranging sentiment in support of a Jewish nation in Palestine. In 1800 James Bicheno wrote his *Restoration of the Jews*; the United States President John Adams declared in 1818: "I really wish the Jews again in Judea, an independent nation." The private secretary to Napoleon III, Ernest Laharanne, argued for a Jewish state in a book published in 1860, and in that same year the Earl of Shaftesbury drew up detailed plans for the settlement of Jews in Palestine under British auspices, which he presented to the government and circulated among Protestant heads of state in Europe and in the United States. The Mormon missionary Orson Hyde was sent to Jerusalem in 1841 where he dedicated the country to the Jews from the top of Mount Scopus. The Italian philosopher and politician Benedetto Musolino insisted that Jewish settlement in the Land of Israel would bring European culture to the Middle East. Jean-Henri Dunant, founder of the International Red Cross, tried in vain, from

Members of Hovevei Zion *(Hebrew: "Lovers of Zion"), a European Zionist movement whose members began to arrive in Palestine in 1882.*

Meeting of the Second World Zionist Congress in Basel in 1898.

1863 to 1876, to get support for Jewish settlement in Palestine. In 1876 the revival of Jewish nationalism was the theme of George Eliot's impassioned novel *Daniel Deronda.*

All these were a prelude to modern Zionism, which grew out of the desire to liberate the oppressed Jewish minority, strengthened by the age-old bond to the Holy Land, and differentiated from the previous yearning for Zion by its predominantly secular outlook.

"Normalized" through Settlement

The Damascus Blood Libel of 1840, when the Jews were accused of the ritual murder of a Capuchin monk, catalyzed the idea that the Jewish People needed to be "normalized" through settlement in the Holy Land. Rabbi Judah Alkalai and Rabbi Zevi Hirsch Kalischer were stimulated to advocate a return to Zion within the framework of traditional religious thought, but also developed some elements of modern nationalism. Moses Hess, on the other hand, did not come from a religious background. In his *Rome and Jerusalem*, published in 1862, he argued that the Jewish problem must be solved through "national ren-

Left: (top) The first settlers at Rishon LeZion; (bottom) the settlement a few years later.

Right: (top) The beginnings of Rehovot; (bottom) aerial view of the research institute at Rehovot Agricultural Station in 1924.

aissance" — the reconstruction of national life based on socialist principles, in the ancient homeland.

These and other thinkers inspired a group known as "Hovevei Zion" (Lovers of Zion — in some countries called "Hibbat Zion") which established societies throughout Europe. In 1882 members of the group began to arrive in Palestine and soon founded numerous settlements and towns, including Rishon LeZion, Rosh Pinah, Petach Tikva and Zichron Ya'akov. By 1885 there were almost 14,000 members organized into 100 societies and five years later the towns of Rehovot and Hadera were established.

Among the leaders of the movement, convinced of its ideology by the pogroms which followed the assassination of Czar Alexander II, was Leon Pinsker. In his pamphlet entitled *Autoemancipation,* which was published in 1882, Pinsker called for "the creation of a Jewish nationality, of a people living on its own soil, the self-emancipation of the Jews . . . as a nation among nations by the acquisition of a home of their own."

Pinsker insisted that anti-Semitism would be solved only by removing all Jews from the Diaspora. On the other hand, Asher Ginsburg, known as Ahad Ha'am ("One of the People") called for the establishment of a Jewish spiritual center in Palestine in order to redeem Judaism.

Leon Pinsker, author of Autoemancipation *in which he called for the establishment of a Jewish national center.*

Visionary of Zionism

The person who took all of these strands and wove them together into a single organization devoted to the return to Zion was Theodor Herzl. Born in Budapest in 1860, Herzl grew up in the Liberal or Reform tradition of Judaism. When he was 18, his family moved to Vienna where Herzl obtained a doctorate in law. He turned to journalism and from 1891 to 1895, served as the Paris correspondent of the Neue Freie Presse of Vienna.

In 1894 Herzl covered the trial of Captain Alfred Dreyfus in Paris. The false accusation of treason against Dreyfus and the subsequent outburst of anti-Semitism, convinced Herzl that the Jews could not be assimilated in Europe. In his slim volume *Der Judenstaat* (The Jewish State) published in 1896, he declared: "We are a people — one people, and the only solution to anti-Semitism is sovereignty . . . over a portion of the globe large enough to satisfy the rightful requirements of the nation; the rest we shall manage for ourselves."

Herzl's noble appearance and the fact that he was an assimilated Jew who had come back to his people, stirred the masses of Eastern Europe. The members of Hovevei Zion and others enthusiastically called on him to lead them and supported his proposal for the convening of a Jewish national assembly.

In August 1897 the First Zionist Congress met in Basel, Switzerland.

Everything was organized to give the impression that it was the parliament of the Jewish People — a newly designed flag, dues called "shekel" (an ancient Jewish coin), a bank (the Jewish Colonial Trust), an official press, and even formal attire required on the part of all the delegates. The Congress established the World Zionist Organization and elected Herzl as its president.

In his diary, on September 3, 1897, Herzl wrote: "In Basel I founded the Jewish state. . . . Maybe in five years, certainly in fifty, everyone will realize it." The words were prophetic. Fifty years later, in November 1947, the United Nations called for the establishment of a Jewish state in Palestine.

Herzl's main goal was a publicly secured homeland for the Jews. In search of this "Charter" he turned to Berlin and Constantinople, meeting both the German Kaiser Wilhelm II and Sultan Abdul Hamid. But these efforts turned out to be fruitless. Herzl turned next to Russia and Britain. During his trip to St. Petersburg in 1903 he was greeted tumultuously by Russian Jewry, but the Minister of Interior's promises of support were never kept.

Great Britain, on the other hand, seemed quite interested and in 1900 Herzl convened the Fourth Zionist Congress in London, hoping that "Great England, free England ... will understand our aspirations." The British government first proposed that the feasibility of Jewish settlement in the area around El Arish in the Sinai Desert be examined, in order to secure the eastern approach to the Suez Canal. The lack of water and arable land, however, put an end to this scheme. In 1903 Colonial Secretary Joseph Chamberlain offered to establish an autonomous Jewish settlement in Uganda. Disappointed by the failure of his other efforts, Herzl told the Sixth Zionist Congress that if the Holy Land was not available, the persecuted Jews should accept any temporary refuge.

On July 3, 1904 Herzl died. Two years earlier he had completed his novel *Altneuland* which outlined a Jewish state in twenty years' time. On the frontispiece were the words: "If you will it, it is no dream."

The Seventh Zionist Congress in 1905 rejected the Uganda scheme and decided that the Zionist Organization would henceforth concern itself only with settlement in Palestine. As a result the "political Zion-

Petach Tikva at the end of the 19th century.

ists" who felt that their goals could only be accomplished by the granting of a "Charter" took second place in the Movement to the "practical Zionists" who saw their rights to the Holy Land as self-evident and insisted on implementing them by immigration, settlement and the development of the land. They supported the efforts of the "Second Aliya" who were achieving these goals in Palestine.

During this period a variety of Zionist parties were established. Some combined Zionism and Jewish religion; others saw socialism as the indispensable handmaiden of Zionism; still others subscribed to the Marxist analysis of society. In any case, the Zionist Movement, on the eve of the First World War, was firmly established both in the Diaspora and in Palestine.

During the First World War a Zionist political campaign slowly began to take place in London. It was headed by Chaim Weizmann, a Russian-born lecturer in chemistry at the University of Manchester. The Zionist idea fell on fertile ground: British Protestants were sympathetic to a Jewish return to Zion; using the Jews to keep the French and Russians far from the Suez Canal suited British foreign policy, and the potential propaganda value of winning over the Jews in America and Russia was not to be overlooked.

The Balfour Declaration

Thus on November 2, 1917 the Balfour Declaration was issued in the form of a letter to Lord Rothschild, stating that "His Majesty's Government view with favour the establishment in Palestine of a national home for the Jewish People, and will use their best endeavours to facilitate the achievement of this object. . . ."

The impact upon Jewish communities throughout the world was electrifying. Weizmann immediately formed a Zionist Commission for Palestine which arrived in the Holy Land in April 1918. One of the first acts of the Commission was to lay the foundation stone of the Hebrew University in Jerusalem. Weizmann also met with the Arab leader, Emir Feisal, and came to an agreement with him promising close cooperation in the development of Palestine. (Unfortunately, Feisal was murdered.)

Article Four of the Palestine Mandate which was granted to Great

(left)
Early days of settlement near Rehovot of Yemenite immigrants.

Guarding the fields. The watchman, Avraham Arieh, was killed on duty by Arab marauders in 1934.

Chaim Weizmann meeting the Arab leader Emir Feisal in 1918.

Britain at the San Remo Conference in 1920 stated that "the Zionist Organization shall be recognized as an appropriate Jewish Agency for the purpose of advising and cooperating with the Administration in matters affecting the Jewish population in Palestine. . . ." Thus during the entire period of the British Mandate the Jewish Agency or Zionist Organization played a key role in the political, economic, social and cultural development of the Jewish community of Palestine.

The Jewish Agency, headed by the President of the World Zionist Organization, had an Executive both in London and Jerusalem. The latter worked closely with the Vaad Leumi (National Council), which had been established in 1920 and was recognized some years later by the Mandatory government as the representative of the Jewish community in Palestine (the Yishuv). The Jerusalem Executive was responsible for land development, immigration, settlement, agricultural research and afforestation. It assisted the National Council in providing health, education and social services to the community. Its Political

Young immigrants in the care of the Youth Aliyah program in 1939.

Youth Aliyah children brought from Eastern Europe through Teheran, Iran, in 1943.

"Teheran children" receive a lesson in planting vegetables.

Department negotiated with the British Palestine Administration on these and all other matters concerning the welfare and security of the Jews.

One of the main instruments of the Zionist Movement in building the homeland was the Jewish National Fund (JNF), established at the Fifth Zionist Congress in 1901. The JNF purchased swamp land and other uncultivated areas and Zionist settlers reclaimed them.

Using the contributions of Jews and Zionists throughout the world, through the Keren Hayesod, which was set up by the Twelfth Congress in 1921, the Jewish Agency helped the development of housing, industry and communications throughout the country. Other Zionist organizations had their specific fields of interest, such as medical services by Hadassah — the Women's Zionist Organization of America, social welfare by WIZO — the Women's International Zionist Organization, and religious education by the Mizrachi Zionists.

With the increasing antagonism of the British Administration towards the development of the Jewish National Home, much of the attention of the Jewish Agency and the World Zionist Organization was taken up with political matters. The 1929 Arab riots led to the

When immigrants arrived at Kibbutz Geva in 1936, they lived in tents until houses were built for them.

promulgation of a White Paper by Lord Passfield, Secretary of State for the Colonies, negating the essential principles of the Balfour Declaration and Palestine Mandate. The Zionist leadership fought this White Paper bitterly and secured the publication of the MacDonald letter, which substantially softened the anti-Zionist implications of the original document. The Arab riots of 1936 led the British government to set up a Royal Commission headed by Lord Peel, which reached the conclusion that it was impossible to meet Jewish and Arab claims in the same territory and recommended the partition of the country into a small Jewish state and a larger Arab one. The Peel Report was debated at the Twentieth Zionist Congress, which was divided on the issue, but directed the Executive to seek an improvement of the proposal. It was, however, rejected completely by the Arabs. When the Second World War broke out, David Ben-Gurion, Chairman of the Jewish Agency

Orphans from Rumania brought by Youth Aliyah in 1946

Executive declared: "We will fight the war as if there were no White Paper [severely restricting land purchase and immigration] and fight the White Paper as if there were no war."

In 1942 the American Zionist Movement, at Ben-Gurion's initiative, organized a conference at the Biltmore Hotel in New York to discuss the problem of Palestine. The resulting "Biltmore Program" called for the establishment of a Jewish Commonwealth in Palestine and was ratified by the Zionist General Council (the supervisory body of the Zionist Executive).

The Jewish Agency represented the Palestinian Jewish community at the United Nations and when the State of Israel was declared in 1948 the Jewish Agency and the World Zionist Organization (WZO) formed the nucleus of the State's new government. Dr. Chaim Weizmann, President of the WZO became the first President of Israel. David Ben-Gurion became Israel's first Prime Minister and numerous other members of the Jewish Agency Executive became Cabinet Ministers. The Political Department was transformed into Israel's Ministry of Foreign Affairs.

Role of WZO Defined

But the establishment of Israel as a sovereign state put into question the future role of the Jewish Agency and the WZO. The problem was quickly solved when it was decided that world Jewry, through these two groups, would help Israel absorb the hundreds of thousands of Jews who decided to return to Zion. In August 1948 the Zionist General Council, meeting in Tel Aviv, decided that the Jewish Agency would organize *aliya* (immigration); receive, accommodate and help employ the new *olim* (immigrants); continue to care for young immigrants through the Youth Aliyah program; settle immigrants on the land; handle land amelioration and afforestation through the Jewish National Fund; enlist support and understanding for Israel and disseminate information on the country; promote the cultural and spiritul association of Jews with Israel and help advance Jewish cultural and educational programs in the Diaspora; stimulate participation in Israel's

The Twenty-third World Zionist Congress convened in Jerusalem for the first time in 1951 and formulated the new goals of the Zionist movement after the foundation of the State of Israel.

An absorption center for new immigrants.

Students from different countries take a break from their intensive Hebrew course at the absorption center.

Russian immigrants arriving in Vienna on their way to Israel in the 1980s.

economic development and organize and guide Zionist youth movements throughout the world.

The Twenty-third Zionist Congress, which met in Jerusalem in 1951, endorsed this program and summed up the new goals of the Zionist Movement in the so-called Jerusalem Program: "The task of Zionism is the consolidation of the State of Israel, the ingathering of the exiles in the Land of Israel, and the fostering of the unity of the Jewish people."

In 1952 the Knesset affirmed the program and in 1954 a formal Covenant was signed by the Government of Israel and the Executive of the World Zionist Organization (the Jewish Agency) recognizing the latter as the body representing world Jewry in relation to the practical functions of *aliya* and the settlement of immigrants.

Thus the Zionist Movement accomplished its original aims: it established a Jewish national movement; revived the Hebrew language and literature; reclaimed and developed the Land of Israel; transformed the character of the people and the land; created an open society, and gave the Jewish People the right to guide its own destiny.

Moreover, having succeeded in establishing a Jewish state and implementing the Return to Zion, Zionism continues to be a vibrant force in Jewish life, strengthening the State of Israel, promoting the ingathering of Jews in their historic homeland, preserving the identity of the Jewish People through the fostering of Jewish and Hebrew education and Jewish spiritual and cultural values, and protecting Jewish rights everywhere.

Government
and institutions
of the State

Israel is a parliamentary democracy whose citizens are guaranteed equality, regardless of race, religion or sex, and freedom of religion and conscience, of language, education and culture, by the Declaration of Independence and the country's laws and traditions.

The President
Although he is the titular Head of State, the President of Israel is largely a figurehead with very little real power. He is elected by the Knesset for a five year term and may serve a maximum of two terms.

The tasks of the President include: the signing of all laws and international conventions, ceremonial functions, such as receiving the credentials of foreign diplomats, appointing Israel's diplomatic representatives, judges, the State Comptroller, the Governor of the Bank of Israel, and opening the first session of a new Knesset; formal functions

David Ben-Gurion, flanked by members of his provisional government, reads Israel's Proclamation of Independence on May 14, 1948 in Tel Aviv.

and the representing of Israel in visits to foreign countries; and a limited number of substantial functions, such as the pardoning of prisoners and the mitigation of sentences (usually on the recommendation of the Minister of Justice), and, after consulting with the representatives of the political parties, calling upon a given Member of the Knesset to form a new government (almost always the leader of the largest party).

The first President of Israel was Chaim Weizmann, formerly President of the World Zionist Organization, who served until his death in 1952. He was succeeded by Itzhak Ben-Zvi (1952–1963) and Zalman Shazar (1963–1973), both Second Aliya pioneers who came to the office at the culmination of a long political career. The fourth President was Professor Ephraim Katzir, a scientist of international renown, who retired from office after one term. In 1978 he was replaced by Yitzhak Navon, formerly political secretary to David Ben-Gurion, who was the youngest President of the country. The current President, elected in 1983, is Chaim Herzog, who had served as a military officer, diplomat and Member of the Knesset.

The Knesset

Supreme legislative authority in Israel rests with its parliament, the Knesset, a unicameral body with 120 members. Members of the Knesset are elected by universal country-wide suffrage, in a secret ballot. All citizens are eligible to vote from the age of 18 and eligible to be elected from the age of 21. The Knesset is elected for a four year term, under a system of proportional representation, but it may dissolve itself and call for early elections. Voters cast their ballots for national party lists

of candidates, with the entire country serving as a single constituency. Knesset seats are allocated according to each party's percentage of the total vote.

The Knesset must approve each new government and its program. If a government loses a vote of confidence in the Knesset, it must resign, although no government in Israel has so far fallen as a result of a motion of no-confidence. The government is constitutionally subject to the Knesset's supervision and control, which it effects through approval of the State's annual budget, by public debates in the plenary, written and oral questions by Members of Knesset to the ministers, and closed discussions in its ten standing committees which hear reports from ministers and other officials.

Plenary debates are open to the public and are conducted in Hebrew, although Arab members may address the house in Arabic, which is translated into Hebrew.

The Presidents of the State of Israel since the proclamation of independence. From left to right: Chaim Weizmann (1948–52), Itzhak Ben-Zvi (1952–63), Zalman Shazar (1963–73), Ephraim Katzir (1973–78), Yitzhak Navon (1978–83) and Chaim Herzog, President since 1983.

The Knesset is presided over by the Speaker and several deputy speakers, who are elected according to party strength. The Speaker, usually a member of the largest party, draws up the agenda based on the government's priorities. There are two sessions a year and three meetings a week. The time allotted to each debate is decided in advance and then divided proportionally among the parties according to size. Seating arrangements are in a series of semi-circles in which the parties sit, from the left, in order of size, with the government occupying the innermost circle.

Opposite page:
(top)
View of the Knesset, Israel's parliament.
(bottom)
The Knesset in session. Members of the government sit in the innermost semi-circle. The Press and distinguished visitors occupy the gallery above, while members of the public view the proceedings from behind a glass panel on the extreme left.

David Ben-Gurion, the first Prime Minister of Israel from 1948 to 1954 and again from 1955 to 1963, when he resigned for "personal reasons."

Constitution and Legislation

The first of the Knesset's laws, the Transition Law of 1949, set out in general terms the powers of the President, the Legislature, and the Cabinet or Government. After a lengthy debate in 1950, the Knesset assigned the task of preparing a constitution to a committee. Each chapter of the constitution was to be a separate Basic Law. Since then, while no complete constitution has been presented to the Knesset, a number of Basic Laws have been enacted.

Besides the normal legislation that is similar to that passed in most other nations, there are a number of laws peculiar to Israel as a Jewish state. Foremost among these is the Law of Return (1950) which recog-

nizes the right of every Jew to immigrate to Israel.

Legislation is generally presented by the Cabinet after being drafted by the Ministry of Justice and the ministry concerned with the subject.

The Government

The Cabinet, headed by the Prime Minister, is Israel's Government and executive branch. Collectively responsible to the Knesset, it is the State's main policy-making body. By law, only the Prime Minister must be a Member of Knesset (MK); in fact, the other ministers are usually also MKs. There is no limit to the number of ministers the Prime Minister can appoint.

The resignation or death of the Prime Minister, the election of a new Knesset, or a successful no-confidence vote lead to the resignation of the government.

Israel's system of proportional representation and the multiplicity of political parties have prevented a single party from receiving a majority of 61 MKs and, therefore, all of Israel's governments have been coalitions. Until 1977 the major partner in these coalitions was the Israel Labor Party, which was the largest party in the Knesset. In the 9th and 10th Knessets, the Likud emerged as the largest bloc and its head, Menachem Begin became Prime Minister. In 1984 elections to the Knesset resulted in a stalemate, with neither the Likud nor the Labor Alignment able to form a government without the other. This led to the establishment of a National Unity Government, with the two blocs agreeing upon the rotation of the Prime Minister between Labor's Shimon Peres (1984–1986) and Likud's Yitzhak Shamir (1986–).

Ministries within the Cabinet are generally distributed in accordance with the coalition agreement. The Prime Minister largely determines

the agenda of the Cabinet which usually meets once a week. The Cabinet submits legislation to the Knesset and sometimes also brings policy decisions to the Knesset for discussion and approval.

The first Prime Minister of Israel was David Ben-Gurion who served from 1948 to 1954 and from 1955 to 1963. Between these two periods Moshe Sharett was Prime Minister. When Ben-Gurion resigned in 1963 he was replaced by Levi Eshkol (1963–1969) who died in office. Golda Meir served next as Prime Minister until 1974 when she was succeeded by Yitzhak Rabin. Menachem Begin served from 1977 until his resignation in 1983 when he was replaced by Yitzhak Shamir until the 1984 elections.

Political Parties

Most of Israel's political parties were founded during the period of the British Mandate or even earlier. Even before the establishment of Israel they vied against each other in numerous elections. The first Knesset election in 1949 was, therefore, basically a continuation of the political scene which had begun almost two decades earlier.

Of the 16 parties represented in the current Eleventh Knesset two —

Opposite page:
(top)
Moshe Sharett, Prime Minister
1954–55.
(bottom, left to right)
Levi Eshkol, Prime Minister
1963–69; Golda Meir, 1969–74;
Menachem Begin, 1977–83.

Arab citizens in Nazareth queue to cast their votes in the first elections to the Knesset in 1949.

Residents of East Jerusalem voting in the 1981 elections.

the Likud and the Alignment — account for more than two-thirds of the 120 members.

The largest component of the Likud bloc is the Herut Movement which was founded in 1948 by Menachem Begin, commander-in-chief of the Irgun underground force, which itself was a product of Vladimir Jabotinsky's Revisionist Movement (founded in 1925). It promotes an activist defense policy, stresses the territorial integrity of the Jewish homeland, advocates private enterprise and emphasizes respect for Jewish religious values. As the major opposition to the Labor Party it was excluded from all coalition governments (with the exception of the National Unity Government after the 1967 War) until it won the 1977 elections.

In 1965 the Liberal Party (successor to the General Zionists and Progressive parties) joined Herut to form the Gahal bloc which became the Likud in 1973. The Liberals maintain a middle class philosophy and advocate a private economy with minimal government interference.

The Labor Alignment is a successor to Mapai, a socialist labor party founded in 1930 by the merger of two other parties established by the pioneers of the Second Aliya at the beginning of the 1900s. Headed for many years by David Ben-Gurion, Labor was the strongest political force in the Jewish community during the Mandatory period, and headed the Government of Israel from 1948 to 1977. It advocates "constructive socialism" based on social-democratic principles.

The Mapam Party, a more leftist political group, which was part of the Labor Alignment until 1984, advocates a socialist economy and the withdrawal of Israel from the territories it has occupied since 1967.

The four religious parties — the National Religious Party, Shass, Agudat Israel and Morasha — emphasize the religious aspects of Israeli life. Until 1977 when it joined the Likud coalition government, the NRP had "a historic coalition" with Labor and was a member of all of Israel's governments.

The remaining parties have four or less seats each. They include the nationalist Tehiya, the extremist Kach led by Rabbi Kahane, the Civil Rights Movement, Change Party, Hadash (Democratic Front For Peace and Equality) dominated by the Rakach Communist Party, Tami — an Oriental Jewish community party and the Arab Progressive List for Peace.

Labor Alignment headquarters after the 1984 Knesset elections Party leader Shimon Peres is speaking on the telephone.

First cabinet meeting of the National Unity Government after the rotation of Prime Ministers in 1986. Prime Minister Yitzhak Shamir is seen, center, with his deputy Shimon Peres on his left.

Meeting of the National Unity cabinet during the premiership of Shimon Peres in 1984.

The Judiciary

The absolute independence of all Israeli courts from the Executive and Legislative branches is guaranteed by law. Judges are appointed by the President of the State, on the recommendation of a public nominations committee, for life and must retire at the age of 70.

The Supreme Court has nationwide jurisdiction. It is the country's highest Court of Appeal on rulings of lower courts. As the High Court of Justice it is able to grant relief in all matters from any jurisdiction in the interest of justice. As such it generally acts on petitions brought by persons seeking redress against administrative decisions by the government, local authorities or other public bodies.

Magistrates and district courts exercise jurisdiction in civil and criminal cases, with the latter the venue of appeal from decisions of the former. Juvenile, traffic, military, labor and municipal courts each deal with matters coming under their jurisdiction. Small claims courts have been established to relieve some of the congestion in the other courts. The religious courts have jurisdiction in matters of personal status of members of their community.

The trial of Nazi war criminal Adolf Eichmann in Jerusalem, 1961. The defendant is in the witness box on the left, flanked by police officers.

There is no jury system in Israel, even though the law is based largely on the British system. One or three judges generally comprise a court and decide all questions of fact and law. Any person may appear in his own defense without legal counsel.

Local Government

Democratically elected local authorities in Israel provide citizens with such services as water, drainage, sanitation, roads, parks and social services, as well as sports, health, educational and cultural facilities. Municipal budgets must be approved by the Ministry of Interior, as must local tax rates, which account for about half of the budget with the government providing the other half.

In 1948 there were a total of 34 local authorities in the country. Today there are over 200, including 40 municipalities (three of which are Arab), 126 local councils (60 Arab) and 53 regional councils.

Since 1978 the mayors and heads of local councils have been elected by direct popular vote. Previously they had been elected by the City Council which is still chosen by proportional representation of party lists — some national and some local. Permanent residents who are not Israeli citizens may also vote in local elections.

The Police

Israel's Police Force is responsible for the maintenance of law and order, crime prevention and traffic control. Israel's police force is also responsible for preventing terrorist acts and infiltration.

The highly trained and mobile Border Guard assists the police in their regular duties, aids the army, and is responsible for maintaining order at the country's airports and harbors, as well as protecting the border areas. A select unit of the Border Guard has been trained to combat terrorism.

The Prison Service is also part of Israel's Police. Its 19 institutions hold criminals, security prisoners and women offenders. Rehabilitation programs include social work and psychiatric services, as well as vocational guidance and training and educational courses.

Police patrol car and motorcycle.

Schoolchildren learn the rules of road safety from a police officer.

Policewoman on traffic control duty.

The Israel Defense Forces (IDF)

The Israel Defense Forces was established on May 26, 1948 by the Provisional Government. However, it was not until several months later that the various underground groups which fought the British were disbanded and the IDF established as the country's sole fighting force.

After the War of Independence the IDF was organized into regular and reserve forces. The reserves constitute some two-thirds of the IDF, with a larger component of regular personnel in the Air Force and Navy than in the Army.

All Israelis from the age of 18 are obligated to serve in the IDF; men for three years and women for two. Married women and Arabs are totally exempt from conscription. Religious girls may request an exemption on the basis of their beliefs (a large number opt for a civilian national service) and yeshiva students are exempt from service while pursuing their religious studies.

Nahal units (Pioneer Fighting Youth) combine their national military service with agricultural work. After basic training, they are assigned under army discipline to frontline villages. These villages or kibbutzim usually become civilian in time, often settled by the original Nahal units.

Hesder units combine religious study with national service. Military training and religious study are interposed for a total of four or five years, rather than the usual three years of service.

Upon conclusion of the period of national service or conscription, every person is assigned to a reserve unit, which has a nucleus of regular officers and men who keep the unit and weapons in combat condition. Men are eligible for reserve duty (usually one month a year) until the age of 55 and women until 34 or until they have a baby. Call-up exercises are held periodically to ensure that the mobilization of the reserves can be effectuated as swiftly as possible.

Between the ages of 45 and 55 men generally serve in Haga or Civil Defense. These units, while including duty patrolling streets and safeguarding public buildings, are designed to cope with attacks on civilian concentrations and also serve in numerous bases and posts on the borders.

Moshe Dayan, Chief-of-Staff of the Israel Defense Forces in 1953–58, who commanded the Sinai Campaign, and Yitzhak Rabin, Chief-of-Staff in 1964–68, commander during the Six Day War.

The Chief-of-Staff is appointed by and responsible to the civilian Minister of Defense and the Cabinet. In addition to the government, the activities of the IDF are supervised by various Knesset Committees. The C-O-S heads the General Staff which includes Operations, Intelligence, Logistics, Manpower and Planning. There are three Regional Commands — Northern, Central and Southern — which are both tactical and territorial, the latter linked with the Jewish settlements along the frontiers.

Officer cadets of the Israel Defense Forces on parade.

A young sergeant salutes.

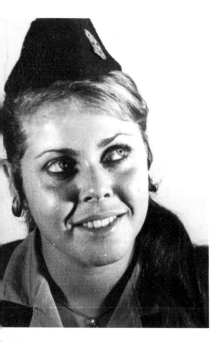

(clockwise from left)
Girl soldier; parade at an Offi-
cers' School; girl soldiers at
camp; soldier returning from
maneuvers.

The three arms of the IDF are the Ground Forces or Army, the Navy and the Air Force. The Ground Forces include infantry, paratroops, armor, artillery, engineers, communications, intelligence, medical services, military police, supply, ordnance, regional defense, Nahal and Haga. The Air Force is considered IDF's elite force, however the Navy has become increasingly advanced and active in recent years and is responsbile for patrolling Israel's sea border.

High technology, one of the main means used by the IDF to overcome its numerical inferiority, is to be found in all branches of the IDF.

Rafael Eitan, Commander of infantry and paratroopers, later Chief-of-Staff (1979–83), inspects newly-promoted officers in 1972.

Israel produces much of its own requirements in the fields of electronic and counter-electronic warfare, surveillance, command and control.

Because of its universal conscription policy, the IDF plays a major social and educational role in Israeli society. It serves as a Hebrew language school and helps merge the diverse elements of the population. Many soldiers learn skills and trades which help them in civilian life. Female soldiers are sent to development towns to teach and assist in social welfare. Special programs are provided for problematic and disadvantaged youth, with basic education courses and apprenticeship schemes for those who do not meet the IDF standards.

IDF arms are either purchased abroad (mainly from the United States) or developed and built in Israel. The Uzi submachine gun, the Galil automatic rifle, the Kfir fighter jet, the Merkava tank and the Gabriel sea-to-sea missile are some of the weapons Israel has developed and produced. It has also improved weapons purchased abroad.

Thus the Israel Government is ramified but well organized. It is democratic at all stages and closely tied to the people. Most important, it has succeeded in knitting together a mosaic of cultures and peoples into a single nation.

Israel's flourishing cities

Tel Aviv — Center of Commerce and Entertainment
Tel Aviv is Israel's second largest city with a population of more than 320,000 at the beginning of 1987. It is the hub of a metropolitan area which houses almost one-third of the country's total population.

While the modern city is less than eighty years old, the city of Tel Aviv is a blend of the old and the new. Archeological explorations have uncovered evidence of prehistoric habitation, as well as the remains of a Philistine town from the 12th century BCE.

On March 11, 1909 representatives of some sixty Jewish families gathered on the sand dunes outside Jaffa. Almost all were Second Aliya pioneers who had decided to build a modern town rather than live in rural settlements. Led by Meir Dizengoff, an Odessa businessman who had settled in Jaffa four years earlier, the pioneers formed two companies — Achuzat Bayit and Nachalat Binyamin — which purchased twenty-eight barren acres simply because the land there had been offered at a reasonable price. That morning the heads of the sixty families drew lots for the plots of land and heard Dizengoff prophesy that the city they were establishing would one day hold 25,000 people — a seemingly impossible dream. They called the new town Tel Aviv, the Hill of Spring, taking the name from the Prophet Ezekiel (3:15) and from the Hebrew title of Theodor Herzl's visionary novel *Altneuland*.

Dancing in the streets of Tel Aviv in celebration of Independence Day, 1969.

Nahalat Binyamin Street in Tel Aviv in the 1920s.

Over the years the small town grew, expanding northward along the coast and eastward. It housed the first Hebrew secondary school in the country, the Herzlia Gymnasium, whose fortress-like structure with towers and arches dominated early Tel-Aviv, until it was torn down in 1969 to make room for the huge Shalom Tower department store and offices. As a result of the Arab Rebellion, 1936–39, a Jewish port was opened in Tel Aviv to compete with the one in Jaffa. The port was closed 30 years later when the port of Ashdod was opened and today the area nearby is a favorite night spot for residents and visitors, with bars, outdoor restaurants and nightclubs providing entertainment until the early hours of the morning.

On May 14, 1948 David Ben-Gurion read Israel's Declaration of Independence to a special meeting of the Vaad Leumi, in the Tel Aviv Museum, which had previously been the home of Mayor Dizengoff. Hakirya, located in what was once Sarona, a German colony established in 1871, became the headquarters of the Provisional Government of Israel and the city served as Israel's temporary capital. Today Hakirya houses the headquarters of the Defense Ministry and the General Staff of the Army.

Today, Tel Aviv is Israel's commercial and financial center. Within the city are the nation's stock market, diamond exchange, headquarters of all Israeli banks, and most of the country's investment and insurance

Rothschild Boulevard, Tel Aviv, in the 1920s.

institutions. Numerous private firms are located in the city, as well as
luxury fashion houses for clothing and furs, representatives of overseas
corporations and importers of consumer and other goods.

The city is an institutional and organizational center, housing the
national offices of the Histadrut, the main offices of the Ministry of
Defense, known as the Kirya, all of Israel's political parties, the kibbutz
movements, as well as numerous world Jewish bodies.

Tel Aviv is an important cultural center. It is the home of Tel Aviv
University (Bar Ilan University is in next-door Ramat Gan), the Tel
Aviv, Ha'aretz and Beit Hatefutzot Museums, most of the nation's
publishing houses, presses and daily newspapers, sports associations,

The first street lamp in Tel Aviv.

The sand dunes on which Tel Aviv was built are still very much in evidence in these early photographs of Rothschild Boulevard (center) and Herbert Samuel Avenue (bottom).

Public transportation, Tel Aviv, 1912.

The Yarkon River at Tel Aviv in the 1920s.

*Violinist Isaac Stern appearing
at the Mann Auditorium, Tel Aviv.*

Habimah Theater.

Tel Aviv Museum.

Beit Hatefutzot, the Diaspora Museum.

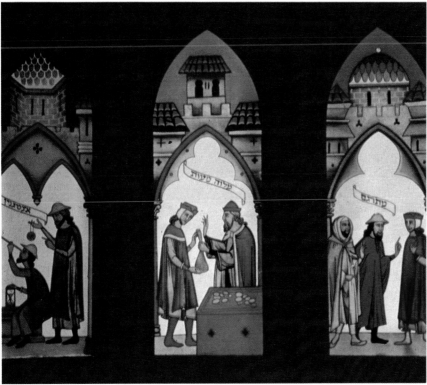

Depictions of Jews in medieval times showing some of their occupations, from left to right: an astrologer, a moneylender and an interpreter. They are part of the multi-media reconstruction at Beit Hatefutzot of Jewish life in the Diaspora through the ages.

as well as the Israel Philharmonic Orchestra, the Habimah Theater, and a variety of other theater and dance companies.

It is also a tourist center with luxury hotels, fine beaches, department stores and shopping centers, a boating Marina, innumerable sidewalk cafés, boutiques and outdoor markets.

Jaffa, the world's oldest port and the place where the prophet Jonah set sail for Tarshish, was merged with Tel Aviv in 1949. It has been restored and is now a picturesque artists' colony with numerous galleries, studios and shops, as well as restaurants and night clubs.

Opposite page:
View of Tel Aviv from the top of
Migdal Shalom

מגדל שלום מאיר

Migdal Shalom, Tel Aviv, one of
Israel's tallest buildings.

This building, constructed in
1925, was Tel Aviv's town hall
until 1965. Today it serves as the
Museum of the History of Tel
Aviv-Jaffa.

The I.B.M. Building (left) and Beit Asia Building, Tel Aviv.

Aerial view of Tel Aviv beach and yacht marina.

View of Jaffa from the sea.

(left)
Restored old houses in Jaffa.

(right)
Tomb of a Muslim saint, Jaffa.

(left)
Restored house in Jaffa.

(right)
*The door of the old caravanserai
(inn for caravans) in Jaffa.*

Haifa — Main Port and Center of Industry

Israel's main port and third largest city (with a population of 223,400 at the beginning of 1987), Haifa lies on the slopes of Mt. Carmel.

Mt. Carmel — "Vineyard of God" in Hebrew — was a synonym for beauty used by Solomon in his Song of Songs. It was here that Elijah waged his struggle with the prophets of Baal, and the discovery of Canaanite shrines on the mountain give physical proof to the religious significance of the site. Additional archeological revelations point to habitation on the hillside as far back as prehistoric times. Conquerors including Alexander the Great, the Romans, the Crusader Tancred and the Mamelukes, destroyed the city, but it was always rebuilt.

Haifa's growth into a modern city began in the 19th century when steamships began using the port. In 1868 the German Templar Society, which believed that the country's material restoration was a necessary prelude to its final redemption by the Second Coming, built fine houses, schools, charitable institutions and roads in the city, and introduced the stage coach. In 1902 Theodor Herzl described Haifa as "the city of the future" in his book *Altneuland*. A few years later the city's development was accelerated by the influx of population when the Haifa–Damascus section of the Hejaz Railway was completed. After the city was taken over by the British in 1918, the railway was extended to Lod and then to Cairo. Jews began to acquire land on the Carmel slopes and in 1920 founded the Hadar Hacarmel quarter. In 1924 the Technion Institute accepted its first students. Ten years later the port facilities were modernized and expanded and just before the Second World War the Kirkuk–Haifa oil pipeline was laid and the Haifa Oil Refineries installed.

View of the Bay of Haifa and the Bahai Shrine in the foreground.

Panoramic view of Haifa

The Technion Campus on Mount Carmel in Haifa.

Haifa by night.

During the war and after, immigration was focussed on Haifa, including the "illegal" immigrants who ran the British blockade and the thousands who entered the country after the establishment of the State. Jewish forces captured the city during the War of Independence and called on the local Arabs to remain and live in peace with them. But egged on by their leaders all but some 3,000 of Haifa's 76,000 Arabs abandoned the city. Today, the 20,000 Arab inhabitants account for some 10% of the total population.

Since 1948 the city has continued to grow. In 1956 the Kishon Port was built to serve Israel's high-sea fishing fleet and the Israel shipyards. In 1963 the University of Haifa was established as a liberal arts center for the Galilee.

The center of heavy industry and international trade and commerce, Haifa has the country's only subway, the Carmelite, which goes up and down the slopes of Mt. Carmel. It is the World Center of the Bahai faith, with the landmark gold-domed Shrine of the Bab surrounded by beautiful gardens. The 22,000 acres of the Carmel National Park comprise one of the largest parks in the country. Elijah's Cave, on the slope of Mt. Carmel is said to be the place where the Prophet fled from King Ahab and is sacred to Jew, Moslem and Christian alike. A labor-oriented city, Haifa is the only one of Israel's large towns where public transportation runs on the Sabbath.

The Horn of Carmel, near Haifa.

Cave of Elijah on the slope of Mount Carmel. According to tradition, the prophet took refuge here from persecution. It is a holy place to Jews, Christians and Muslims alike.

The caves of Wadi Mughara in the Carmel range near Haifa which were inhabited by man in prehistoric times.

Beersheba — Gateway to the South

The "capital of the Negev" goes back almost 6,000 years in history. It was first settled in the Chalcolithic period (around 4000 BCE) by farmers who raised cattle. Their jewelry, pottery, stone vessels, basket-work and figurines, carved out of ivory and bone, which have been uncovered by archeological explorations, show how highly developed was their craftsmanship.

Beersheba, however, is best known from the Bible. Its name — "Well of the Oath" or "Well of the Seven" — is derived from the seven ewes Abraham set aside as a sign of the covenant made on oath between himself and Abimelech, King of Gerar. Isaac and Jacob lived there and it was later part of the territory of the tribe of Simeon, the southern border of the country.

It was one of the cities settled by the Jews when they returned from Babylonian exile, and during the Roman period it was the center of a series of fortresses designed to protect the country against the neighboring Nabateans. Many remains of this period have been found, including mosaic floors, Greek inscriptions and the inscription of an ancient synagogue. The Crusaders erected a fortress in the town, which may have been the reason that Beersheba was destroyed some time during the period the Arabs ruled the country.

In 1880 the city was rebuilt by the Ottomans who laid a railroad line from it to the coast and later extended it into Sinai. In 1917 it was captured by General Allenby, but during the entire period of the British Mandate it remained undeveloped, occupied mainly by wandering Bedouin and those who profited from their regular market.

When Egypt attacked Israel in 1948 Beersheba was quickly overrun and served as a major Egyptian base. In October 1948 Israel launched an operation to ensure that the Negev become part of the Jewish State and Beersheba was captured by the Israeli Army.

In the past forty years Beersheba has grown to a city with a population of 115,000 inhabitants, representing a cross-section of Jews from all over the world. The original "Wild West" frontier town flavor of the first years of statehood has disappeared with the city's growth, but the weekly Thursday morning Bedouin market remains one of the few reminders of that era. Today it houses the flourishing Ben-Gurion University of the Negev, with a School of Medicine and over 5,000 students, and the Institute for Arid Zone Research which investigates the

Remains at the site of biblical Beersheba.

effect of the desert environment on man, the development of water desalination, the exploitation of solar energy, artificial rainmaking and the more efficient use of the Negev's natural resources.

Beersheba is also the gateway to both the Negev and the Dead Sea, the latter with its health spas and chemical plants. In the Negev, the largest and least populated area of Israel, a number of development

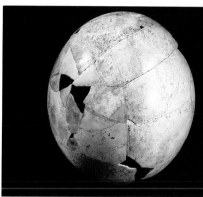

towns have been established, experimental farms which are making the desert flourish by irrigation and conservation of the meager rainfall, and Sde Boker where Israel's first Prime Minister David Ben-Gurion chose to make his home upon his retirement. There are many kibbutzim in the area as well as those of Gush Katif, south of the Gaza Strip, populated by former Israeli settlers in the Sinai before it was returned to Egypt in 1982, following the signing of the peace treaty.

(clockwise from left)
Remains of storerooms at the site of biblical Beersheba.

Pot from biblical Beersheba inscribed with Hebrew letters.

Ostrich egg from the Persian period found at the same site.

Churn for making butter dating from the Chalcolithic period in Beersheba.

Beersheba Muncipal Museum.

Open-air market in Beersheba.

View of Beersheba.

Eilat — Thriving Southern Port

Israel's southernmost city has only recently awakened from centuries of slumber. Eilat was first mentioned in the Bible as the point at which Moses and the Children of Israel turned away from the direct route to the Promised Land to wander in the desert for forty years. Almost a century later King David staked his furthest defense line around the city when he conquered the southern Negev.

It was, however, during the reign of Solomon that Eilat (also known as Etzion Geber) developed the most. David's son made it the home port for his fleet which traded with Arabia and Ophir, exchanging the Negev's minerals for gold and spices. It was Solomon also who developed the nearby copper mines, still visible today, and it was the wise King of Israel who brought the Queen of Sheba to his capital by way of the thriving southern port.

But the end of the united kingdom also ended the prosperity of Eilat which saw a succession of conquerors in the following centuries. The Edomites, the Egyptian Ptolemies (who named it Berenice), the Nabateans, the Hasmoneans, the Romans (who called it Aila), the Byzantines, the Arabs who used it as their base for the invasion of the Holy Land, the Crusaders who built a fortress on a small island just off the coast (whose remains are still intact), the Mamelukes, the Ottomans and the British all controlled the city in turn.

The Turks built a port a few miles away and named it Aqaba (now Jordan's outlet to the Gulf), while the British built a police station at the site called Umm Rashrash.

The 1949 Armistice Agreement with Egypt gave Israel the entire Negev down to the Sinai border. To ensure its control over the area Israel sent two infantry columns who, on March 10, 1949, reached the three abandoned huts of Umm Rashrash, raised the Israeli flag and restored the name Eilat.

For eight years some 500 hardy Israelis who made their home in Eilat bore their isolation stoically. They were more than 200 km. from Beersheba and nearly 350 km. from Tel Aviv and all their supplies had to be trucked in. But the 1956 Sinai Campaign changed all that. With the opening of the Gulf of Aqaba to Israeli shipping, the route to Asia and Africa lay open.

(left)
Prototype of the ships that sailed to Tarshish in the time of King Solomon to bring iron, silver, tin, and lead.

Remains of Crusader fortress on Coral Island, off Eilat.

Today the city's nearly 23,000 inhabitants are served by a modern airport as well as a modern highway. The port, built in 1974, serves ships which reach East and South Africa, Southeast Asia, the Far East and Australia. The pipeline from Eilat to Ashkelon on the Mediterranean coast moves oil from tankers to Israel's cities. Industries such as fishing, jewelry, and ceramics are slowly developing.

Eilat is now a major tourist center. Its balmy weather all year round (amost never dropping below 10°C even in the winter) and the beautiful tropical sea with its unique coral reefs, sea-sport facilities, fine beaches and hotels have made it a popular resort for both Israelis and tourists from all over the world. In November 1985 Eilat was declared a Free Trade Zone and, as the first stage, declared exempt from payment of Israel's 15% Value Added Tax.

Eilat's coral reefs, inhabited by innumerable species of exotic tropical fish, attract skin- and scuba-divers from all over the world. The reefs may also be viewed from glass-bottomed boats or from the underwater observation chamber of the Aquarium.

View of Eilat. A plane is about to land at the airport.

Yacht marina at Eilat.

View of Eilat from the sea.

The capital: Jerusalem

Capital of the State of Israel, the City of Jerusalem is unique among the cities of the world — historically, religiously and politically.

Its most outstanding characteristic is its appeal to millions of people: Jerusalem has been the center of the Jewish faith for almost three thousand years. It has been the capital of a Jewish state three times.

Jerusalem is the site of Christ's crucifixion, his resurrection and ascension. It is the symbol for the heavenly Jerusalem.

Jerusalem is "the first of the two *qiblas*" — the original direction of Muslim prayer; the place from where the angel Gabriel took Muhammad to heaven on a winged steed.

Jerusalem is a place of contrasts. It is here, on the watershed, that the Mediterranean landscape turns into the Judean Desert. It is here that East meets West and Arab meets Jew. It is here in the Holy City that modern urban life exists side by side with the holiness and ancient traditions of the three religious faiths.

These contrasts give the city its special character. They fuse into a single unity, and without them Jerusalem would cease to be herself.

View of Jerusalem from the Mount of Olives. In the foreground is the Old City with the golden Dome of the Rock in the center. Towering in the background are the tall buildings of the New City.

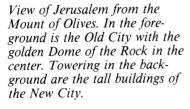

The Ophel, north of the City of David, is seen to the left. On the right of the picture is the village of Silwan.

The Early Days

Jerusalem predates written records. By the time of the biblical Patriarchs, or the Early Bronze Age, the city is already well-known among the established settlements of Canaan. Genesis calls it "Salem" and describes how the Patriarch Abraham was welcomed by its king, Melchizedek, who "brought forth bread and wine . . . and blessed him." The Egyptian Execration Texts of the 19th–18th centuries BCE refer to it as "Rushalimum." A few centuries later, in the 14th century BCE (the Late Bronze Age), the El-Amarna clay tablets, inscribed in cuneiform letters, contain messages from Abdi-Hiba, "King of Urusalim." The Book of Joshua, referring to the same period, explains how the Israelites went to war to capture the city but could not hold it against its Canaanite inhabitants, the Jebusites.

Canaanite Jerusalem was located on the slopes of a hill called the Ophel, south of the present-day Old City. Surrounded by steep valleys, it was naturally defended and the supply of water was ensured by the Gihon Spring, which still exists today. The some 4,000 inhabitants of

In the center of the Dome of the Rock on the Temple Mount is the Even Shetyya *(in Hebrew, "the foundation rock"). In Jewish legend it is the focal point of the world, or "the rock from which the world was woven," on which stood the altar of the Temple which King Solomon built.*

the city were mainly farmers who supplemented their income by providing hospitality and services to the merchants who passed by. They maintained their independence by exploiting the city's strategic importance: Jerusalem lay on the junction of the major roads bisecting the country, leading from Egypt in the south to the nations of the Tigris and Euphrates Rivers in the north, and it separated the tribal areas of Judah and Benjamin. In this "foreign enclave" they built retaining walls to strengthen the terraces upon which they constructed their homes. They also established a holy place, which probably had a lengthy tradition as an altar, on a hill to the north of the city.

General view of the City of David, with the excavations on the left, the El Aksa mosque on the right and the city walls in the background.

The City of David

Around the year 1000 BCE David, King of Israel, decided to create a national capital for his newly united kingdom. Having defeated the House of Saul after a long civil war, David chose Jerusalem, still under

foreign control, to consolidate his position. The Bible relates that David and his men captured the Jebusite stronghold by entering the city through the tunnel leading up to the Gihon Spring.

The King, moving his residence into Jerusalem, gave it the status of the royal domain and the capital of the realm. He embarked upon a vast building program and constructed a huge citadel called the "Stronghold of Zion," a name which would later become synonymous with the city and the country and would be the inspiration for the Zionist Movement which reclaimed the land for the Jewish people three thousand years later.

David also brought the Holy Ark of the Lord into the city, making Jerusalem more than the administrative center of the kingdom; henceforth it would be the religious center of the people of Israel. He erected an altar on "the threshing floor of Araunah the Jebusite" which tradition has placed on Mount Moriah, the site of the Jebusite holy place and the spot where Abraham prepared to sacrifice his son Isaac. It was not, however, David but his son Solomon who was to build the Temple on this site.

Four years after he ascended his father's throne, in 965 BCE, King

View of Mount Zion. At the summit is the Dormition Church and Abbey, to the right, the city wall.

Solomon began construction of the Temple of the Lord. Seven years were devoted to the building of what became known as the First Temple, a small but splendid edifice whose spiritual inspiration would last for centuries.

Monument in the Kidron Valley, known as the Monument of Absalom, held by tradition to be the site of King David's rebellious son's burial place.

Solomon also devoted much energy to building up Jerusalem. In the area between the City of David and the Temple Mount he created a huge palace, thus expanding the city. Jerusalem was transformed from a small town into the center of a large and powerful kingdom.

The First Return to Zion

The city stood thus for more than 350 years. After Solomon's death the country was divided into the Kingdoms of Judah and Israel and Jerusalem became the capital of the former. Under Kings Uzziah (8th century BCE), Hezekiah and his son Manasseh (7th century) the city developed and expanded, spreading westward. In 700 BCE Hezekiah built a new tunnel to bring the water of the Gihon Spring into the city. Twenty-five centuries later, in 1880, the tunnel was uncovered and the Siloam Inscription, carved by Hezekiah's workmen, was revealed.

Tablet recording the reburial of the remains of King Uzziah, between the 1st century BCE and the 1st century CE. Found on the Mount of Olives, it reads: "Hither were brought the bones of Uzziah, King of Judah. Do not open."

During these years Jerusalem was the home of the Prophets of Israel — Isaiah, Jeremiah, Ezekiel and others — who preached their unique message of social justice and righteousness to the Kings of Judah and the people. Then, in 587 BCE, the Babylonian army led by King Nebuchadnezzar captured the city, destroyed the Temple and exiled the inhabitants to Babylon. For five decades the exiles longed to return to their city and country. The wish became reality when Cyrus, King of Persia, conquered Babylon and allowed the Jews to return to Zion. The Temple was rebuilt and under Ezra and Nehemiah the religious, spiritual, political and economic life of the Jews in their land was reconstructed. Soon Jerusalem was again thriving.

Wall painting dating to the 3rd century CE at the synagogue of Dura-Europas portraying Ezekiel's vision of the dry bones.

Hellenization and Revolt

In 332 BCE Alexander the Great conquered Syria and Judah. Jerusalem, reportedly, surrendered without a fight and Alexander did not interfere with Jewish autonomy. This autonomy continued under the Ptolemies of Egypt and Jerusalem prospered as the administrative center of Judah, with the Temple's High Priest as religious and political leader.

However, in 198 BCE the Seleucid King Antiochus III, ruler of Syria, wrested the Holy Land from the Ptolemies. The Hellenization of Jerusalem began with the gymnasium rivalling the Temple as the city social center. Antiochus IV, who ascended to the throne in 175 BCE, decided to wipe out Judaism, plundering the Temple and desecrating it with a statue of Zeus and the sacrifice of a pig on the altar. The Jews revolted, led by the Hasmoneans, Mattathias and his sons, with Judah Maccabee the eldest. After three years of fighting, in 164 BCE the Maccabees purified and rededicated the Temple. Twelve years later they governed Jerusalem and established the Hasmonean Kingdom, whose capital expanded and prospered becoming the religious, commercial and scholarly center for the Jews of the Diaspora, as well as of the Holy Land.

Roman Rule — Aelia Capitolina

For one hundred years no external enemy menaced Jerusalem, but internal strife tore the city apart and led to the end of its independence. The struggle between the Pharisees and the Saducees and the war of

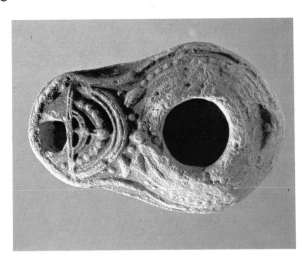

Oil lamp from the Second Temple period.

succession between the sons of Alexander Yannai, brought the intervention of the Romans. In 63 BCE Pompey captured Jerusalem, setting the Hasmonean king on his throne as the vassal of Rome and ending Jewish independence.

Twenty-six years later Herod, backed by the Romans, captured Jerusalem and became King of Judea. A bloodthirsty tyrant, Herod was also a master builder and outstanding administrator. He rebuilt the Temple into a magnificent structure and constructed palaces and buildings in Jerusalem and throughout the country. He made the city and Judea a major center of commerce and used Roman technology to greatly improve the agriculture of the country. His reign was marked by prosperity. But riots and rebellions followed Herod's death in 4 BCE, and the ruling Roman Procurators became more and more strict. During this period Jesus lived, taught and was crucified in Jerusalem.

In 66 CE the Jews revolted against Rome, and for three years ruled an independent Jerusalem until it was conquered by Titus in the year 70 CE and the Second Temple destroyed on the 9th of the Hebrew month of Av, which to this day is marked by fasting and reading the Book of Lamentations. Sixty years later the Emperor Hadrian decided to rebuild Jerusalem as a Roman city named Aelia Capitolina and erect a new Temple — to the Roman god Jupiter. This decision helped spark a new Jewish revolt led by Simon Bar Kochba. Jerusalem was freed, but again only for three years before it was recaptured by the Romans in 135 CE. Aelia Capitolina, built in the form of a square Roman camp, remained a quiet provincial city for almost two hundred years.

Byzantine and Arab Rulers

When Constantine, the Christian Emperor of Rome, defeated the Eastern Roman Empire in 324 CE, he became ruler of the Holy Land. Two years later his mother Helena visited Jerusalem and at her behest Con-

Pompey, the conqueror of Jerusalem in 63 BCE.

(right)
(clockwise from left)
A coin of Herod the Great; coin issued by Pontius Pilate; coin struck by Bar Kochba, leader of the Jewish revolt in 132 CE; the so-called Judaea capta *coin.*

Pillar commemorating the Tenth Roman Legion in the Old City.

stantine began to transform the city into a Christian center, building the Church of the Holy Sepulcher, the Church of the Ascension and others. Additional churches were built by the Empress Eudocia in the 5th century and by the Emperor Justinian in the 6th century.

Jewish control of Jerusalem was regained briefly when the Persians conquered the city in 614, but returned to the Christians after three years when the Persians withdrew their support of the Jews.

In 638 Caliph Omar and his Muslim army conquered Jerusalem. Muslim rule was benevolent and Jerusalem even prospered under the Umayyad dynasty from Damascus. Caliph Abd al-Malik of that dynasty built the splendid Dome of the Rock on the Temple Mount in 691 and his son Walid built the Mosque of El-Aksa nearby. The Umayyads also constructed a huge palace and five other buildings just outside the Temple Mount, strengthened the walls of the city and reconstructed some of the gates within the walls. However, when they were replaced by the Abbasid caliphs from Baghdad in 750, the city gradually began to decline.

The Dome of the Rock, built by caliph Abd al-Malik.

Capital of the Crusader Kingdom

The Crusaders captured Jerusalem in 1099 and, after massacring the Jewish and Muslim inhabitants, made the city the capital of their kingdom. For a while the city flourished as the focal point of Christendom, with tens of thousands of pilgrims visiting the holy sites, the construction of new churches and religious institutions, and the repair of the city's defenses and older churches. But diminished European interest weakened the Crusaders and they were defeated by Saladin in 1187. Forty-two years later they returned to Jerusalem but civil war and the lack of a strong leader depleted their strength and in 1244 the Tartars sacked Jerusalem, massacred the Christians and ended the Crusader rule of the city.

(left)
The Pool of Bethesda in the Old City of Jerusalem with the foundations of a Byzantine church and the remains of the Crusader church which was built on its ruins.

(right)
Facade of the Church of the Holy Sepulcher.

Mamelukes and Ottomans Embellish the City

From 1250 Jerusalem was ruled by the Mamelukes, slaves who had been conscripted into the Egyptian army and eventually overthrew the Ayyubid Empire founded by Saladin. Under their reign Jerusalem again experienced a period of intensive building. The Dome of the Rock and the El-Aksa Mosque were extensively repaired, the majestic Cotton Gate, chapels and public drinking fountains were built, theological schools were established, complete streets restored and repairs made to the city's aqueducts. However, the two minorities were frequently persecuted and heavily taxed. By the end of the 15th century there were only 10,000 inhabitants in the city.

In 1517 Jerusalem was captured by the Ottoman Turks whose rule was to last exactly four hundred years. Fifteen years later Suleiman the Magnificent began to rebuild the walls of the city, which still surround the Old City. He remodelled the Dome of the Rock, constructed the so-called Sultan's Pool as an additional water reservoir, placed public fountains throughout the city and repaired the Citadel. But with his death in 1566 construction in Jerusalem halted and the city's development ceased. The Ottoman Empire began to decline; Jerusalem was of little interest to the central authorities in Constantinople and local authorities were either corrupt, powerless or both. Jerusalem sank to a low ebb in the 17th and 18th centuries.

Damascus Gate with the causeway built to span the archeological excavations below.

(left)
The tombs of two Turkish notables at Jaffa Gate. According to legend, these are the graves of the two engineers charged with building the city walls who were executed by order of the sultan for leaving Mount Zion and the Tomb of David outside the wall.

(right)
Inscription in Arabic on the facade of Jaffa Gate commemorating its construction in 1538 by Suleiman the Magnificent.

St. Stephen's Gate, also known as the Lions' Gate because of the two pairs of lions carved on its facade.

(left and right)
Renovated courtyards in the Jewish Quarter of the Old City.

Modern Development

The 19th century saw a change in the city's fortunes as a result of renewed interest on the part of the European Powers in Jerusalem's holy places. The Christian nations began to care for the various churches under their protection and provide them with funds. Foreign consuls were active in the city and promoted a wide range of missionary and charitable activities. In 1848 the first bank was opened and the first post office by the Austrians. The first Hebrew book was published in the city in 1841 and six years later the Latin Press was established, followed by the Armenian and Greek Orthodox. In 1854 two Jewish hospitals were opened. Modernization quickened and the population grew. In 1860 the first Jewish quarter, Mishkenot Sha'ananim was built outside the Old City walls by Sir Moses Montefiore a British, Jewish philanthropist. That same year Ludwig Schneller, a German Protestant priest, built an orphanage further northwest. A carriage road between Jerusalem and Jaffa was completed in 1868 and more Jewish quarters built in the "new" city. Noted archeologists came to explore the past

(left)
Shunei Halahot Street in the Jewish Quarter.

(right)
The Butchers' Market in the Muslim Quarter.

Some well-known spots in the New City (clockwise from left): a house built in the late 19th century; the Windmill built by Sir Moses Montefiore in 1858; some of the apartments at Mishkenot Sha'ananim, the first neighborhood to be built outside the city walls; the former Palace Hotel, built in the late 1920s, which now houses the Ministry of Commerce and Industry.

and Kaiser Wilhelm of Germany came to visit in 1898. Zionist pioneers added impetus to the revitalization of the Jewish community.

The First World War desolated the city with almost a third of the population fleeing because of arrests, conscription, famine and epidemics. In December 1917 Turkish rule ended when Jerusalem surrendered to the British Army led by General Allenby.

For the first time in centuries, Jerusalem was once more a capital city, seat of the British Government of Palestine and the headquarters of the Zionist Executive. The city developed rapidly, physically expanding to the north and the south, but mainly to the west. Between 1921 and 1935 a new Jewish neighborhood was established almost every year. In 1925 the Hebrew University was dedicated on Mt. Scopus. A new Government House was built in 1931, the Jewish Agency compound in 1932 and the Hadassah Hospital in 1938 on Mt. Scopus. The population grew from 62,500 in 1922 to 165,000 in 1947.

Jerusalem's development, however, was accompanied by clashes between Arabs and Jews. In 1920 Arab mobs killed five Jews in the city

(left)
Kiryat Wolfson, a complex of modern high-rise apartments on a hill overlooking the Valley of Rehavia in the New City.

(right)
The Generali Building, constructed for an Italian insurance company in 1934 and surmounted by its winged-lion symbol. It now houses government offices.

(left)
The headquarters of the Jewish Agency for Israel, the World Zionist Organization, the Keren Kayemet Le-Israel (Jewish National Fund) and the Keren Hayesod (Foundation Fund).
(right)
The residence of the President of the State of Israel.

(left)
The tower of the Y.M.C.A. building, designed by Q.L. Harmon, architect of the Empire State Building in New York, and constructed between 1928 and 1933.
(right)
Hechal Shlomo includes a synagogue and the headquarters of the Chief Rabbinate of Israel.

(left)
View of the Israel Museum.
(right)
Replica of the Liberty Bell of Philadelphia, commemorating the Declaration of Independence of the United States on July 4, 1776. The public garden in which it is displayed was dedicated on the bicentennial of this event.

(left)
King David Hotel. One of its wings, used as British headquarters, was blown up by the IZL (underground resistance organization) in 1946, but has since been rebuilt.
(right)
The L.A. Mayer Memorial Institute and Museum of Islamic Art.

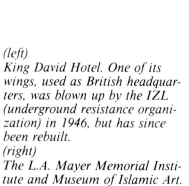

and wounded more than two hundred. In 1929 six Jews, including a Rabbi and his two children, were killed and prayer books at the Western Wall destroyed. During the "Arab Rebellion" between 1936 and 1939 thirty-six Jews were killed in Jerusalem.

During the Second World War Jerusalem became a military headquarters and the British and the Jews cooperated against the common German enemy. When the threat receded in 1944, the underground Jewish groups renewed their attacks on British troops to force them to leave the country. In July 1946 the IZL (underground resistance organization) blew up British headquarters located in Jerusalem's King David Hotel and the city was soon divided into British, Arab and Jewish zones. The situation worsened after the United Nations approved the Partition Plan in November 1947, with the Arabs rejecting it and the British refusing to cooperate in its implementation. Jerusalem lapsed into anarchy. Bombs destroyed the offices of the English-language newspaper the "Palestine Post," blew up a block of houses on Ben-Yehuda Street in the center of town and destroyed part of the Jewish Agency building. Between November 1947 and April 1948 almost three hundred Jews were killed in the city and on roads leading to it.

Capital of the State of Israel

When the British troops left the country and the State of Israel was established on May 14, 1948, Jerusalem was cut off from the rest of the country by the Arab villages lining the road from the coast, water supply to the city was interrupted, food was rationed, electricity and fuel were almost non-existent, and both Mt. Scopus and the Jewish Quarter of the Old City were isolated from the rest of Jerusalem. Two weeks later the inhabitants of the Jewish Quarter surrendered to the soldiers of Jordan's Arab Legion.

But the Israelis managed to repulse all attacks on the New City and in June broke the siege of Jerusalem by opening the "Burma Road," an alternative makeshift road to the coast. The fighting ended with the Old City and East Jerusalem in the hands of the Jordanians, while the New City, surrounded on three sides by Arab-controlled territory, remained in Jewish hands. The Armistice Agreement signed by Israel and Jordan in April 1949 formalized this division, with barbed wire and concrete walls cutting through streets and neighborhoods. Moreover, for the next nineteen years the Jews were denied access to their

(left)
View of the Hebrew University campus on Mount Scopus.

Ben-Gurion Government Center, a complex housing the offices of the Prime Minister and of several other Ministries.

Holy Places in the Old City, as well as the use of the Hebrew University and Hadassah Hospital on Mt. Scopus, despite Jordan's commitment to allow free passage to them.

Nevertheless, Israeli Jerusalem grew. Its population which had dropped to 84,000 in November 1948 increased to 197,000 at the beginning of 1967; more than 50,000 immigrants had moved to the city between 1948 and 1951. A new Hadassah Medical Center was built in Ein Karem and a new campus of the Hebrew University at Givat Ram. The Government Center, with office buildings for the major ministries, was constructed nearby, next to the new Knesset building. The Israel Museum was completed in 1966 and Hechal Shlomo, the seat of the Chief Rabbinate, was erected in the center of town. On Mt. Herzl a national cemetery for Israeli and Zionist leaders was established, with a military cemetery on one side and Yad Vashem, the national memorial to the victims of the Holocaust, on the other. The Ministry of Foreign Affairs moved to Jerusalem in 1953, as the President's office had done a few months earlier. New neighborhoods were established throughout the city and in 1959 Teddy Kollek was elected Mayor. Thus, on the eve of the Six Day War, Jerusalem was a pleasant but sleepy town, the capital of Israel but hardly its center.

Some of the monuments at Yad Vashem, the national memorial to the Holocaust Martyrs and Heroes:
(left)
Memorial to the child martyrs by Moshe Safde.
(right)
"Korczak and the Children of the Ghetto" by Boris Sakstier. In the background can be seen the "Pillar of Heroism" by Buki Schwartz.

The Avenue of the Righteous Among the Nations commemorates persons and organizations who helped save Jews from the Nazis.

Divided City United

On the morning of June 5, 1967, when war broke out between Israel and Egypt, Prime Minister Levi Eshkol transmitted an urgent message to Jordan's King Hussein stating that Israel "will initiate no action in the Jordanian sector unless Jordan attacks us." In response Jordan began firing upon New Jerusalem, first with small arms and then with mortars and artillery. At 1:00 p.m. Jordanian troops crossed the Armistice Line and captured the United Nations headquarters on Government Hill. Israel counterattacked, driving the Jordanians back, and in the next two days, linked up with the isolated Mt. Scopus, broke into the Old City regaining control of the Temple Mount and the Western Wall, and capturing all of Jerusalem and the West Bank.

For those Israelis who crossed the old dividing line, the joy at being able to pray at the Western Wall was marred by discovering that the synagogues and schools in the Jewish Quarter had been destroyed and the ancient Mount of Olives cemetery had been desecrated. On June 28, the Knesset approved the reunification of Jerusalem and passed a law protecting the holy places of all the faiths and guaranteeing free access to them. Two days later the barriers dividing the city came down, the gates of the Old City were reopened and roads were repaired. After nineteen years Jerusalem was again a united city.

In the more than twenty years since then, Jerusalem has regained its place as the center of the country. Its population has increased two and a half times from 197,000 in 1967 to some 480,000 at the end of 1987. although part of this increase was due to the incorporation of 60,000 Muslims and Christians at the time of reunification, Jerusalem is the fastest growing major city in Israel and since 1975 it has been the country's largest city.

(left)
The new plaza outside Damascus Gate.
(right)
A garden planted with palm trees, part of the "green belt" encircling the Old City, separates the pedestrian walkway to Jaffa Gate from the busy main road which skirts the city wall.

(left)
Interior of Yohanan Ben Zakkai Synagogue, one of a complex of four Sephardi synagogues in the Jewish Quarter restored after the Six Day War.
(right)
The reconstructed arch of the Hurva synagogue in the Jewish Quarter of the Old City.

Seven new neighborhoods have been built for young couples, new immigrants and those entitled to improved housing. Three of the neighborhoods extended the built-up area of the city and connected it to Mt. Scopus. The other four, two in the north and two in the south, are large suburbs, built at a distance from the existing city but still within its boundaries. Altogether, the thriving new neighborhoods house some 120,000 residents. In addition, another massive housing project, designed for a further 120,000 persons, is presently being built

(left)
Hadassah Hospital on Mount Scopus. In the foreground is "The Tree of Life," the last work of sculptor Jacques Lipshitz.
(right)
The Teachers' Training Seminary in Beit Hakerem suburb.

(left)
View of Ramot Allon, one of the new suburbs of Jerusalem.
(right)
The Sultan's Pool, originally a reservoir for winter rains, has been turned into an amphitheater for outdoor performances. The spotlit city wall, in the background, serves as a natural backdrop to the stage.

in the north. Over 4,000 buildings have been constructed in the Arab sector.

The neglect and destruction of the previous two decades has been repaired. On Mt. Scopus the Hebrew University campus has been expanded and rebuilt, as has been the Hadassah Hospital which in 1978 opened a modern 500-bed medical center. The Jewish Quarter of the Old City has been almost completely restored, with most of the destroyed synagogues reconstructed, new apartment buildings erected and others reconditioned, and various archeological sites uncovered during the construction, restored and opened to the public. The ancient gates of the Old City have been renovated and rubble removed from the city walls, on top of which the Ramparts Walkway has been created. The infrastructure of the Old City has been overhauled and a number of important Christian buildings have been repaired. Surrounding the Old City, the 600-acre Jerusalem Gardens National Park has been created as a green belt to protect historical Jerusalem.

As a result of the city's physical development, its cultural activities have also increased greatly. The Jerusalem Center for the Performing Arts includes the 950-seat Sherover Theater, the Henry Crown Symphony Hall which is the home of the Jerusalem Symphony Orchestra, the Rebecca Crown Auditorium and a Little Theater. Other facilities, many of which occupy what used to be "no-man's land," are the Jerusalem Music Center, the Sultan's Pool Amphitheater, the Khutzot Hayotzer Arts and Crafts Center, as well as the Jerusalem Khan Theater, and the Liberty Bell Garden with its open-air activities.

The Jerusalem Foundation has implemented more than 1,000 varied projects through donations from the friends of the city abroad, ranging

View from the Promenade at East Talpiot, laid out during the 1980s. On the right, in the background, is Mount Scopus; in the center, the Temple Mount; in the foreground, to the left, are the City of David excavations, and to the right the village of Silwan.

The Town Hall.

from the restoration of synagogues, churches and mosques, the establishment of community and youth centers, to the planting of hundreds of public parks and gardens and support for numerous educational and cultural programs.

Jerusalem today, capital of the State of Israel, is a thriving metropolis concerned with the welfare of its residents and dedicated to the preservation of its heritage.

Foreign relations

For the forty years of its existence, the State of Israel has conducted its foreign relations in the shadow of its struggle for survival. The constant enmity of the neighboring Arab States, often supported by violent actions and all too frequently bursting into open warfare, has understandably colored Israel's relations with other nations and international organizations.

As with many other aspects of the Jewish State, Israel's foreign relations began before the State itself was established. In 1947 the Jewish Agency, representing the Jewish community of Palestine, waged an intensive effort to secure support for the proposed United Nations resolution establishing a Jewish state. Members of the Jewish Agency's Political Department — which later became the Israel Ministry of Foreign Affairs — participated in the General Assembly debate. Their endeavor succeeded when the resolution partitioning Palestine into a Jewish and an Arab state was adopted by 33 votes in favor to 13 opposed, and 10 abstentions.

When the State of Israel was proclaimed some six months later, on May 14, 1948, the Arab attacks on the Jews took a new turn with the invasion by the regular armies of Egypt, Jordan, Iraq, Syria and Lebanon, as well as volunteers from Saudia Arabia, Libya and Yemen.

After almost a year of fighting, the Arabs, defeated and war-weary, agreed to meet Israel on the Isle of Rhodes. Under the auspices of Acting UN Mediator Ralph Bunche (an American), Egypt, Lebanon, Jor-

U.N. mediator Ralph Bunche (right) talks to Abba Eban, the Israeli delegate, before the opening of the U.N. Security Council Session on Palestine in November 1948.

The first United States Ambassador to Israel presents his credentials in March 1949.

dan and Syria signed armistice agreements with Israel between February and July 1949. Each of these agreements stated that its purpose was to "facilitate the transition from the present truce to permanent peace."

Nevertheless the Arabs insisted on maintaining a state of war with Israel. An Arab boycott of all Israeli goods and of all companies trading with Israel or investing in the Jewish State was put into effect. Egypt closed the Suez Canal first to Israeli shipping and then to the shipment of goods to Israel via third parties, despite a Security Council resolution calling for an end to the illegal blockade. Nor did the Arabs limit themselves to non-violent actions. Between 1949 and October 1956

Israel's first envoy to the Soviet Union, Golda Meir, presents her credentials in Moscow in May 1949.

there were 11,873 instances of Arab sabotage and violence in Israel; 1,335 Israelis were killed or wounded.

Egypt had begun to actively support terrorist groups (known as *fedayun*) in 1954 and encouraged them to infiltrate across the border to sabotage and kill. In September 1955 Egypt signed an arms agreement with the Communist bloc, providing for the massive influx of Soviet weapons into the area and giving Egypt a 4 to 1 military superiority over Israel. On October 24, 1956 Egypt, Jordan and Syria announced the formation of a joint military command directed against Israel. Five days later, Israeli troops moved into Sinai to wipe out the *fedayun* bases, forestall a combined attack by the Joint Command, and to remove the blockade of the Gulf of Aqaba.

In March 1957, in acordance with United Nations resolutions, Israel withdrew from the Sinai Peninsula and the Gaza Strip in exchange for promises that the Gulf of Aqaba would remain open to Israeli shipping. A United Nations Emergency Force (UNEF) was stationed on the Egyptian–Israeli border and at the Gulf.

Foreign Affairs Minister Golda Meir, head of the Israeli delegation to the U.N., talking with U.N. General Secretary Dag Hammarskjold at the General Assembly meeting in 1959.

For the next ten years, although President Nasser continued to insist that he was at war with Israel, the border between Egypt and Israel remained relatively quiet. On the other borders, however, fortified Syrian positions on the Golan Heights regularly fired on Israeli settlements below them in the Galilee and terrorist activity across the Jordan River resumed with 11 Israelis killed in 1965 and 1966.

On May 14, 1967 Egypt began moving massive forces into Sinai towards Israel. A few days later Nasser ordered UNEF out of Egypt and announced the blockade of the Gulf of Aqaba. On May 30 Jordan signed a military pact with Egypt, placing its army under the command of the Egyptian Chief-of-Staff. Iraq joined the pact on June 4. When efforts by Western powers to stop the march to war failed, Israel, on June 5, 1967, moved to break the stranglehold. The IDF destroyed the Egyptian air force, advanced into Sinai and quickly reached the banks of the Suez Canal. In response to Jordanian fire on the New City of Jerusalem, Israel took control of the Old City and the West Bank. In the north, Israel met the Syrian attack by scaling the Golan Heights and capturing them.

The first German Ambassador to Israel (left) presents his credentials to President Zalman Shazar in 1965.

Immediately after the Six Day War, Israel again offered to make peace with the Arabs. Its hopes were dispelled by the Arab declaration, formulated at Khartoum in August 1967: "No peace with Israel; no negotiations with Israel; no recognition of Israel." Moreover, in 1969 Egypt announced that it no longer considered itself bound by the 1967 cease-fire agreement and began the massive bombardment of Israeli positions across the Suez Canal. More than 260 Israelis were killed in the year-and-a-half long so-called War of Attrition which ended in August 1970 by a United States arranged cease-fire.

Three years later, on Yom Kippur (the holiest day of the Jewish year) in October 1973, Egypt and Syria launched a simultaneous surprise attack on Israel. Egypt crossed the Suez Canal and Syria advanced into the Golan, almost reaching the Jordan River. Israel, after mobilizing its reserves, repelled the invaders and when a cease-fire ended the war eighteen days later, the IDF had recrossed the Canal, isolated the Egyptian Third Army and had recaptured the Golan Heights.

The Yom Kippur War marked a turning point in Egyptian–Israeli relations, since Egypt felt, on the one hand, that it had redeemed its honor, and, on the other, that there was no military solution to the Arab–Israel conflict. Egyptian emissaries met directly with Israelis for the first time in almost thirty years, negotiating an exchange of prisoners, a separation of forces and an Interim Agreement under which Israel withdrew from certain areas in Sinai in return for Egypt's promise to refrain from the use of force and allow the passage of non-military Israeli cargo through the Suez Canal.

Egyptian President Anwar Sadat took his country a step further on the road to peace when he came to Jerusalem in November 1977. Prime Minister Begin subsequently flew to Ismailia and direct negotiations between various levels of Israeli and Egyptian officials took place in Cairo, Jerusalem and Washington, culminating in a 13-day meeting between Begin, Sadat and United States President Carter at Camp David, Maryland in September 1978 which produced a framework for peace in the Middle East and a framework for the conclusion of a peace treaty between Egypt and Israel.

In March 1979 the Egyptian–Israeli Peace Treaty was signed, the two countries exchanged ambassadors and a slow process of normalization began. The assassination of President Sadat in 1981 and the recall of the Egyptian Ambassador from Tel Aviv in 1982 slowed the peace process. Even the return of the ambassador in 1986 and the continuing travel of Israeli tourists to Egypt have not given normalization a renewed impetus. However, Egypt has refused to yield to the pressure of other Arab states to abandon the treaty with Israel and it serves as a major breach in the wall of Arab hostility and as a beacon of light for others to follow.

The Camp David Accords allotted a major role to Jordan in negotiations over the future of the West Bank and the Gaza Strip. They called for a five-year autonomy plan to be followed by a permanent solution for these areas. While Jordan's King Hussein officially rejected the Accords, he and Israeli leaders have tried to find a formula which will allow the two sides to negotiate. These efforts have not yet borne fruit, but the two countries maintain an unofficial relationship which includes the passage of persons and goods across the Jordan River over

First exchange of ambassadors between Israel and Egypt in February 1980:
Israeli Ambassador Eliahu Ben Elissar (center) with President Sadat in Cairo.

Egyptian Ambassador Sa'ad Murtada presents his credentials to President Yitzhak Navon.

the Allenby and Adam Bridges, payments by Jordan to officials in the West Bank, the operation of a Jordanian bank in Nablus since 1986, and other aspects of cooperation between Israel and Jordan.

No such cooperation exists with Syria, which has continued to encourage terrorists, leading the "rejectionist front" against any agreement with Israel, and striving to attain military parity with Israel.

The main obstacle to peace, however, is the terrorist Palestine Liberation Organization (PLO), whose National Covenant calls for the elimination of Israel and the establishment of an Arab–Palestinian state in all of Palestine, and which has, over the years, carried out attacks on Israeli and Jewish civilians abroad. Although recognized by the Arab States as the "sole legitimate representatives of the Palestinians," the PLO has often come into conflict with various Arab countries, including open warfare with Jordan in 1970 and with Syria in 1983.

By 1982 the PLO had, in effect, established a state within a state in Lebanon, controlling large areas of that country, establishing military bases in Southern Lebanon which were used to launch attacks against Israel, and shelling Israeli towns in the northern Galilee. Forced to defend its civilians, Israel launched Operation Peace for the Galilee in June 1982, destroying the PLO infrastructure in Lebanon and forcing the terrorists to leave the country. Although Israeli forces withdrew from Lebanon in 1985, a security zone was established adjacent to the border with IDF troops aiding the South Lebanon Army to keep the terrorists away from Israel.

The United States and Israel

Eleven minutes after the State of Israel was proclaimed in 1948, President Harry Truman announced that the United States had extended diplomatic recognition to the new state. This act symbolizes the com-

U.S. President Lyndon Johnson meeting Israeli Deputy Premier Yigal Allon and Ambassador Yitzhak Rabin.

mon democratic heritage and the bonds of sympathy which link the two countries. These bonds have grown stronger over the years with the United States gradually assuming the role of Israel's major arms supplier and economic and political supporter. America has also become more and more actively involved in the search for a peaceful solution to the Arab–Israel conflict.

U.S. President Lyndon Johnson meets Israeli Prime Minister Levi Eshkol in Texas.

The relationship between the two countries has not always been smooth and differences of opinion have frequently arisen. In 1957, for example, President Eisenhower took the lead in pressuring Israel to withdraw from Sinai after the 1956 War. In 1967 the United States refused to recognize Israel's action of reunifying Jerusalem, and in 1978 the Carter Administration decided to sell fighter planes to Saudi Arabia and announced that it favored "self-determination" for the Palestinians.

On the other hand, President John Kennedy in 1961 guaranteed Israel's security for the first time and a year later sold Israel a major defense system, the Hawk anti-aircraft missile. In 1967 President Lyndon Johnson rejected every call at the United Nations for Israel to give up the territory it occupied as a result of the Six Day War. In 1973

Washington came to Israel's aid during the Yom Kippur War with a massive airlift of military equipment. During the years that followed Secretary of State Henry Kissinger was largely responsible for the series of agreements between Egypt and Israel that culminated in the Camp David Accords, held under the auspices and with the active involvement of President Carter.

During the past forty years, the United States and Israel have developed a "special relationship" with American support preventing Israel from becoming isolated in the international arena. Israel, on its part, is a strategic asset for the United States and a Western outpost in the Middle East.

Israel and Europe
The nations of Europe have traditionally maintained close ties with Israel — political, economic and cultural — since supporting the estab-

French President Charles de Gaulle speaks with Prime Minister David Ben-Gurion during his official visit to France in 1960.

lishment of the state. There have, however, been increasing disagreements concerning a solution to the Arab–Israel conflict.

Relations with Great Britain were strained during Israel's first years because of the former's role as Mandatory Power and it was not until April 1950 that Britain recognized Israel. In 1956 Britain, together with France, cooperated with Israel in the Sinai Campaign, attempting to restore international control of the Suez Canal. Britain also played a leading role in the drafting of Security Council Resolution 242 after the Six Day War which called for peace in the Middle East by terminating all acts of belligerency and Israeli withdrawal from part of the territories occupied in the War. Subsequently British policy moved closer to the Arab position of complete Israeli withdrawal, negotiations with the PLO and Palestinian self-determination. Despite these disagreements, the two countries were united in their opposition to terrorism, have exchanged high level official visits and maintain growing trade relations.

French President Francois Mitterand at Yad Vashem memorial to the Holocaust victims during his state visit to Israel in 1982.

Israel has developed a close relationship with France almost from the establishment of the state; France was Israel's main arms supplier in the 1950s and its partner in the Sinai Campaign. However, on the eve of the Six Day War General Charles de Gaulle declared an arms embargo on Israel. After the War France's policy became more and more pro-Arab and relations were worsened in 1969 when Israel smuggled five gun boats it had paid for out of Cherbourg, and in 1975 when France released the PLO terrorist Abu Daud, who had taken part in the Munich massacre of 11 Israeli sportsmen. Relations have since improved under President Mitterand, who made an official state visit in 1982 (Premier Jacques Chirac visited in November 1987), and trade, scientific and technological exchanges between the two countries have steadily increased.

Relations between Israel and West Germany began only in 1953 when Germany agreed to a restitution agreement with the State of Israel and to pay reparations to individual victims of Nazi persecutions. In 1960 Premier David Ben-Gurion and Chancellor Conrad Adenauer met in New York and Germany began giving Israel secret military aid. Arms sales stopped in 1965 in response to Arab pressure, but that same year diplomatic relations were established between Germany and Israel. High-level visits on both sides took place in subsequent years; Germany is now Israel's second largest trading partner. Tourism, cultural and scientific relations have thrived and cooperation in the production of arms and military equipment is reportedly at new heights.

Israel's relations with the European Economic Community (the Common Market) began with a limited agreement in 1964. This was followed by additional agreements in 1970 and 1975, the latter establishing a free trade area for industrial products. Negotiations are presently underway to safeguard Israel's agricultural exports to the EEC, which were endangered by Spain's entry to the Market. Some 30% of all of Israel's exports go to the EEC countries. Political relations between Israel and the EEC are not as calm as the economic. A number of statements by EEC members have supported the Palestinians' right to self-determination and have called for the PLO to be part of peace talks.

The "Freedon Train", an Israeli demonstration of solidarity with Soviet Jews refused permission to emigrate to Israel, 1986.

(bottom left and right)
Students from Africa and Latin America taking part in agricultural courses.

Students from Africa receiving diplomas from the Hebrew University-Hadassah School of Public Health and Community Medicine.

The Soviet Union and Israel

Although the Soviet Union was one of the first countries to recognize Israel, having supported the 1947 United Nations Partition Resolution and sent crucial military supplies through Czechoslovakia during the War of Independence, relations between the two countries soon deteriorated. Israel's pro-Western alignment almost automatically put it into conflict with the Soviet Union, which gradually increased its support of the Arabs. In June 1967 the Soviet Union broke off relations with Israel and they have not been renewed until now.

Aside from global issues and the East–West conflict, the main topic on the agenda between the two countries is the plight of Soviet Jewry. Israel insists that those Jews who wish to emigrate be allowed to do so and that the cultural and religious rights of those Jews remaining in Russia be protected. The Soviet Union has used the matter of emigration as a card in its negotiations with the United States, allowing Jews to leave when it seeks to obtain concessions from America or when the relations between the two super powers are friendly, closing the gates at other times.

In 1987 a low-level Soviet mission visited Israel to deal with Russian church property and proposals have been made for a renewal of diplomatic relations.

Israel and Africa

Soon after nations in Africa gained independence, and following the opening of the Gulf of Aqaba to Israeli shipping in 1956, Israel established relations with 32 African states and began to develop an intensive program of technical cooperation with these developing countries. Over the next seventeen years almost 3,000 Israeli experts and technicians went to African countries to provide technical assistance, help establish joint projects and companies, and to prepare local personnel to administer and man these projects. During the same period, thousands of persons from these countries came to Israel to participate in a wide range of training programs.

Following the Yom Kippur War almost all the African states yielded to Arab pressure to break relations with Israel. However, the disappointment of African leaders with unfulfilled Arab promises of huge

financial aid, as well as the Israel–Egypt peace treaty, brought about a slow renewal of diplomatic relations. Zaire was the first to resume relations in 1982, followed by Liberia in 1983, the Ivory Coast and Cameroun in 1986. At present seven African states have full diplomatic relations with Israel, while interest officers represent Israel in five more states and negotiations are proceeding with an additional eight countries.

Thus, despite the enmity of its Arab neighbors, Israel has made a breakthrough to full peace and has maintained cordial relations with 70 nations of varying political and economic structures. It is a recognized member of the international community, trading and cooperating with the majority of the countries of the world.

(top and bottom)
African students studying opthalmology at Hadassah Medical Center.

Economy

Israel's economic life during its first quarter of a century, from 1948 to 1973, was characterized by two distinctive features — a tremendous growth in population and an average annual rise in the Gross National Product (GNP) of 10%.

The country's economy has always been influenced by the fact that it has few natural resources and only 25% of its land area is arable — much of that dependent upon scarce water for irrigation.

Thus, the economy was traditionally agragrian. While trade and commerce were important components of the Holy Land's economic affairs at various periods, from the beginning of the Common Era to the end of the 19th century the country lived on a subsistence economy, undeveloped and barely productive.

The beginning of Zionist resettlement of the land in 1878 saw the start of the gradual transformation of the country's agriculture and the rest of its economy over the next 70 years. Mixed farming based on

Irrigation has made possible the reclamation for agriculture of much of the arid lands of the south.

Drip irrigation equipment, pioneered by Israel, being manufactured in a kibbutz factory.

intensive cultivation and irrigation was introduced. Modern technical methods and high capital investment led to a fivefold increase in the export of citrus between 1927 and 1937. Industry more than tripled in the same period.

On the eve of statehood in 1948, following the boom years of the Second World War, industry had expanded and now included metalwork, diamond-polishing and food-processing. Commerce and banking, import and export had been stimulated by the war and the know-how of the Zionist immigrants. An organized working class had emerged and there was full employment. Agricultural production (both cooperative and private) had doubled.

The War of Independence, continuing security needs and the nearly 700,000 immigrants who came to Israel in the first three years of statehood, strained the country's economy almost to breaking point. Employment, food and housing had to be supplied to the nearly penniless immigrants. Unemployment was high; food and clothing were rationed, and because housing was largely unavailable the newcomers lived in tents.

On the other hand, highly-skilled labor and very high motivation made rising production possible. Large amounts of capital flowed into the country as gifts from world Jewry, economic aid from the United States, and loans. Exports, particularly citrus, grew rapidly. Industrialization was heavily supported by the government. By 1952 the construction industry had progressed to meet the demand for new homes, schools and factories, thus beginning to solve the most pressing problems, including unemployment.

Two years later the absorption of the immigrants and their transformation into a productive segment of the society was well underway. In the ten years between 1954 and 1964 West German reparations gave the economy an additional stimulus; the value of agricultural production increased by more than 500% and production per capita more than doubled; foreign currency reserves rose from almost nothing to

(clockwise from right)
Packing roses for export; intensive cultivation of vegetables in a kibbutz greenhouse; mechanical harvest of avocados on a kibbutz.

Seamstresses at work in a textile factory at Dimona.

Weaving at one of the country's largest textile concerns.

Modern food processing plant.

Diamond cutter at work.

The Dead Sea Works, a major
world supplier of potash, bro-
mides and a variety of chemicals,
fertilizers and minerals.

over $700 million; more than half the cost of imports was covered by exports (as compared to 16% in 1949), and nearly 6,000 industries employed over 220,000 persons. The expanding products — both for export and local consumption — included citrus, Dead Sea minerals, cotton, chemicals, pharmaceuticals, precision instruments, electronics, fashion goods, furs and diamonds. Israelis had a much higher standard of living.

The years 1964 to 1967, however, saw a recession throughout the country as a result of inflationary pressures and the import surplus. The government cut back on development and imports to reduce the balance of payments deficit and unemployment reached 10%, immigration fell off, investments and output slowed and private consumption fell.

The recession ended in the aftermath of the Six Day War in 1967. Employment was again full and both production and private consumption rose. Immigration from the United States and other Western countries increased and Soviet Jews began to arrive. Tourism became a major industry with almost 800,000 tourists arriving in the country in 1972. The annual consumption of electricity increased from 5,000 million Kw/h in 1969 to 7,200 million in 1972. Industrial production rose by 29% in 1968, 16% in 1969, and 12% in 1970–72.

At the same time the economy began to overheat. The shortage of labor drove up prices and wages. Inflation was 12.9% in 1971, 14.2% in

A new factory for the manufacture of galvanized pipe fittings.

Metal works at Ramle.

1972, and 26.4% in 1973. The import-export deficit rose to $1,250 million in 1970. As a result the Israeli pound (lira) was devalued by 20% in 1971.

The Yom Kippur War of 1973 and the world energy crisis, which raised the price of oil almost fivefold, had a harsh effect on Israel's economy. The three weeks of warfare cost Israel the equivalent of a year's GNP. The defense budget rose from 16 billion Israeli lirot in 1974 to 22 billion in 1975 and to over 50 billion in 1976 and 1977, almost half the national budget. The country's foreign currency deficit, which was $1 billion in 1973, soared to $8.5 billion in 1976, with the accumulated balance of payments deficit at over $9 billion that year.

Rising world prices for oil, meat, sugar, wheat and other commodities contributed to increase Israel's inflation, which reached an annual rate of almost 50%. In response, the government persuaded the United States to increase its aid fourfold between 1972 and 1974, to almost $2 billion a year, raised gross taxation to around 45% of the GNP, devalued the lira, and reached an agreement with the workers and industrialists on prices and wages. By the end of 1976 inflation was down to less than 30% and the civilian import surplus had been reduced by more than $500 million to $1.7 billion. The economy, however, slowed down and unemployment rose.

In 1977 the new Likud Government effectuated a 60% devaluation and instituted a substantial relaxation of foreign currency controls. It did not, however, reduce government spending and a sharp inflationary trend resulted, rocketing from almost 50% in 1978 to over 110% in 1979 and 445% in 1984. The foreign debt grew by leaps and

A collection of coins and tokens, from the 4th century BCE to the modern State of Israel.

Banknotes from the Turkish period to the 1970s.

bounds and the balance of payments deteriorated rapidly. In January
1983 the Tel Aviv stock market, which had been soaring, collapsed,
and in October of that year, the bank stocks collapsed.

The government reintroduced foreign currency restrictions and wage
and price controls in 1983 but it was not until July 1985 that the
National Unity Government was able to effectuate a tight monetary
policy, sharp budgetary cuts, a break in the link between wages and the
cost of living index and, in January 1986, replacement of the shekel
(which had replaced the lira) with the New Shekel (at a rate of 1,000 to
1) stabilized at 1.5 per US dollar.

The freeze was gradually thawed as wages were allowed to catch up
from December 1985 to February 1986 when a gradual defreezing of
prices and goods and services was begun, and by the end of 1986 about
60% of price controls were lifted. The emergency plan had achieved its
goals: inflation declined from 445% in 1984 to 185% in 1985 and
19.7% in 1986; the rate of unemployment remained relatively stable (at
7.1% at the end of 1986); the budget deficit was reduced to about 4% of
the GNP as the government cut subsidies on food and transport and
imposed new taxes on foreign travel, cars and property; the balance of
payments improved and the Bank of Israel's reserves increased by 60%.

In January 1987 the government moved to the second stage of the
program and a series of comprehensive measures were adopted: the
value of the shekel was lowered by 10%; price increases were approved
on some subsidized goods; a temporary 2.7% moratorium on cost-of-

Fashion show, 1988.

Fashion show, 1949. Paula Ben-Gurion, wife of the Prime Minister, is seated in the front row of the audience, third from the right.

living increases was imposed; reduction of employer social security payments was extended; price controls were extended to the end of March 1988; tax reforms went into effect in April 1987 reducing the top rate for individuals from 60% to 48% and for companies from 67% to 55%; fees on vehicles, contracts, documents, airplane tickets were cancelled (the tax on flights abroad was raised to 250 shekels, but was no longer index-linked); a levy of 3% was imposed on credit in foreign currency received by Israeli residents.

The 1987 budget approved by the Knesset reached a total of 37.6 billion shekels (IS), composed as follows: ordinary budget — IS 11.7 billion; development budget IS 1.7 billion; debt service IS 16 billion; defense budget IS 8.2 billion.

Despite the difficulties, the second stage of the economic stabilization plan seems to be meeting with success due to the fact that it has been most comprehensive, having dealt with inflation, the balance of payments, the budget, tax and capital-market reform and growth.

Agriculture

Agriculture is one of Israel's brightest success stories. The revolution begun by the Zionist pioneers in the 19th century has continued, with the country becoming self-sufficient in most of its food needs and the remaining imports more than financed by agricultural exports.

Agricultural exports rose from $130 million in 1970 to $193 million in 1974, $386 million in 1977 and over $560 million in 1986. In 1985/86 Israel's food production was valued at more than $2.4 billion. This increase in production is mainly a result of technology and mechanization, together with a decrease in the number of agricultural workers. In 1958 15.7% of the labor force was employed in agriculture. This figure dropped to 11.5% in 1963, 9.7% in 1969 and 5.3% in 1986.

At the same time the country's cultivated area rose from 412,000 acres in 1948/49 to 1.1 million acres in the mid 1980s. Almost half of this area is under irrigation, utilizing the National Water Carrier which brings water from the north to the arid south, as well as such unique methods as drip-irrigation which Israel developed in the 1960s. Vegetables and flowers are grown in hot-houses and under plastic, adding to the country's out-of-season exports.

Industry

Despite the lack of raw materials, Israel's industry has become increasingly ramified and productive. Almost one-quarter of the labor force is employed in industry, which accounts for about 20% of the country's GNP.

In 1986 industrial exports reached nearly $6.5 billion. Nearly 30% of this amount came from polished diamonds, an industry in which Israel accounts for almost 40% of the world market. Another 12% of exports was accounted for by chemical products, including various mineral products (potash, bromine and phosphates) extracted from the Dead Sea.

Traditional industrial branches include food production, textiles and fashion (which began in the 1950s), furniture and metal products. High technology, including electronics, telecommunications, computer software and others, was stimulated by the Six Day War, and now comprises more than 10% of both total industrial production and industrial exports.

Basic scientific and technological research is carried out by the institutes of higher education, which are also engaged in applied research

The first locomotive in Palestine, during the Ottoman period.

Waiting area at Lod Airport (now Ben-Gurion Airport) in 1949.

Departure lounge at Ben-Gurion Airport in the 1980s.

and development in coordination with industry and agriculture. Science-based parks have been established in close proximity to universities and research centers to facilitate practical interaction. Defense research is carried out by industry, with extensive governmental support. The Israel Aircraft Industries, the country's largest enterprise, controls a number of concerns making or assembling civilian and fighter jets, trainers, executive aircraft, naval craft and missiles, etc. It has even developed its own fighter plane, a project which was cancelled in 1987 mainly due to lack of finance.

Kibbutzim throughout the country have undergone a rapid process of industrialization. More than 300 kibbutz factories manufacture processed food, irrigation systems, agricultural machinery, plastics, furniture and clothing, bringing in about half of their total revenue and accounting for about 5% of the total production.

Tourism
Tourism has become one of the country's main industries and generates an annual revenue of $1 billion. Over 1.2 million tourists came to visit Israel in 1985, as compared to some 450,000 in 1970. Of these more than half came from Europe, about a third from North and South America, and almost 10% from Asia and Africa. There are nearly 30,000 rooms in over 300 recommended hotels throughout the country and a chain of 32 youth hostels.

Labor Force
The total civilian labor force aged 14 and over is some 1.4 million persons. Of these 37.5% are women. Almost 30% are employed in public and community services, nearly 10% in finance and business services, over 23% in industry, 12.5% in commerce and restaurants, and around 6% each in personal services, agriculture, transportation and construction.

The Histadrut, General Federation of Labor, is Israel's main trade union. Founded in 1920, it is not only the largest representative of the country's workers, but also one of its major employers.

Histadrut (General Federation of Labor) headquarters in Tel Aviv.

Membership in the Histadrut is open to all workers, including house-wives, and it negotiates on their behalf wage and working condition agreements with the government and national employers' associations. Separate unions throughout the economy represent individual factories or fields and professions through elected committees and councils.

Kupat Holim, the country's largest health fund, provides comprehensive medical care to all Histadrut members. In addition, the Histadrut operates a broad network of social and cultural services, including day care centers, convalescent homes, hospitals and clinics, pension funds and publishes a daily newspaper, "Davar."

Through its holding company, Hevrat HaOvdim, the Histadrut owns one of the country's three largest banks (Bank Hapoalim), a construction company (Shikun Ovdim), farm marketing and production (Tnuva), department stores and supermarkets (Hamashbir) and cooperative bus companies (Dan for Greater Tel Aviv area and Egged for urban and inter-urban travel). It is second only to the government as the largest owner of economic enterprises in Israel, employing some 20% of the labor force and accounting for a similar amount of the net domestic product.

International Trade

Israel's exports currently reach $7 billion a year, while its imports amount to over $9 billion (as compared to $530 million and $760 million respectively in 1967). Its main trading partner is Europe which accounts for more than half of its imports and over a third of its exports. The United States, with whom Israel has recently signed a

One of the branches of Bank Hapoalim.

Free Trade Agreement, buys about a third of Israel's exports while selling to Israel a similar percentage of its imports. Israel has been granted preferences under the Generalized System of Preferences (GSP) by Australia, Austria, Canada, Japan, Finland, New Zealand, Norway, Sweden, Switzerland and the United States.

Energy

Oil, the main source of Israel's energy, must be imported. In 1985 fuel imports cost some $1.5 billion, as compared to less than $650 million in 1975. Electricity, the manufacture of which accounts for about one third of fuel imports, reached a total production of over 15 billion kw/h in 1986, of which some 30% were consumed by industry. Total installed generating exceeded 4,000 mgw, including a number of power units fueled by coal to save import costs. Some 25% of all households in Israel are equipped with solar water-heating systems, manufactured locally. Israel is one of the world's leaders in solar energy research and development, and a number of companies in the country have developed such equipment for industrial use, whose manufacture or know-how is exported abroad.

(left)
Foreign journalists at work in the Press Center.

Solar energy provides the power for this ultra-modern street lamp.

Transport and Communications

Over 8,000 miles of roads in the country carry more than 800,000 private cars, trucks and commercial vehicles, with the length of roads doubled since 1960 and the amount of vehicles increased tenfold.

Israel Railways provides passenger service between Jerusalem, Tel Aviv, Haifa and Nahariya. The number of passengers using the railroads has declined in recent years but freight usage has increased. Freight services operate mainly in the southern part of the country, to the port of Ashdod, Ashkelon and Beersheba, and the mineral quarries south of Dimona.

El Al, Israel's national airline ranks high in terms of operational scope among the members of the International Air Transportation Association; it flies a considerable part of the passenger traffic through Ben-Gurion international airport and the balance is flown by foreign

Opposite page:
(top)
View of hotels on the shore of the Sea of Galilee.
(bottom)
Dizengoff Shopping Center, Tel Aviv.

airlines on scheduled flights. Airports at Eilat and Atarot, near Jerusalem, serve international charter flights and internal airlines operate services between the main towns, as well as to the north and south.

Of the country's three ports, Haifa in the north is the oldest and Eilat is the newest. The port of Ashdod accounts for almost half of the more than 16 million tons of freight loaded and unloaded annually. At Ashkelon, near Ashdod, there is a tanker port and Hadera has an off-loading facility for coal supplied to the nearby power station. Zim, Israel Navigation Company, founded in 1945, is the national shipping line.

Over 1.3 million telephone lines service Israel's citizens, connected to over 200 exchanges. In addition there are over 6,000 telex machines and some 7,000 data transfer lines.

* * *

In summary, over the past forty years Israel has created a flourishing, modern industrialized economy, despite the lack of natural resources, the enmity of its neighbors requiring continual mobilization of segments of the work-force, and the absorption of hundreds of thousands of refugees. It has also, in recent years, overcome the tremendous pressure of inflation. The economy has often responded to outside pressures with a downturn, but it has managed to persevere with the basic growth reasserting itself and the country proceeding with its development.

Tourist development at the hot springs at Tiberias on the shore of the Sea of Galilee. The springs' healing effects together with the warm winter climate make Tiberias, 215 m. (700 ft.) below sea level, a popular year-round resort.

New promenade beside the Dead Sea, the lowest spot in the world, 394 m. (1,292 ft.) below sea level. The water is so saline that it is impossible for bathers to sink and its therapeutic properties bring relief to visitors suffering from skin conditions.

Education
and culture

Almost every third Israeli is a student. In the 1986/87 school year 1,401,396 students were registered in more than 7,000 educational institutions — from kindergartens through universities — in all parts of the country.

In the small Jewish community of Palestine in the 19th century, education was centered around the traditional religious schools. Secular education began in the 1950s and 60s with the establishment of modern schools by philanthropic individuals or organizations. With the immigration of the Zionists these schools began to teach in Hebrew and new Hebrew-speaking schools were established. During the Mandatory period parallel but separate Arab and Jewish school systems developed. The Arab system, taken over from the Turks, was attended by mainly Muslim students while the Christian Arabs received their education in missionary or denominational schools. The Jewish system, maintained by the Vaad Leumi (the National Council), consisted of three "trends" — General, Mizrachi and Labor — in addition to a variety of Orthodox schools and *yeshivot* (religious academies).

Thus, when the State was declared, a fully functioning network of schools already existed in the country. Two major pieces of legislation reorganized this system. The first (in 1949) provided for compulsory and free education of all youth, regardless of sex or religion, from 5 to 14 years of age (the mandatory age limit was raised to 16 in 1978). The

Herzlia Secondary School, Tel Aviv, in the 1920s.

second law, in 1953, provided for the transfer of the schools from the former sponsoring organizations to the government. The government system, however, retained the varying outlooks of education so that parents have the choice of sending their children to state schools, state-religious schools, or government-recognized independent religious schools. The state and state-religious schools offer similar academic curricula, with the latter placing extra emphasis on Jewish studies and observance and separate premises and instruction for boys and girls. The independent schools are affiliated with various Orthodox Jewish groups and provide more intensive religious education. Some schools have been established to cater for specific trends, such as Conservative Judaism and the principles of open education. Some three-quarters of the children attend the state schools, about 20% the state-religious schools and the remainder are enrolled in the independent schools.

Israel's educational system includes one year of compulsory kindergarten (from age 5), eight years of elementary and four years of high school, or six years of elementary and three years each of junior high and high school. In addition, private nursery schools prekindergartens, technical, vocational and agricultural institutes, military preparatory schools, teachers' colleges, and universities serve the educational needs of Israelis.

Some 220,000 Arab and Druze (the latter separated from the former

Storytime at a kindergarten in the 1980s.

in 1978) students were enrolled in the Arab educational system in 1986/87. The language in this system is Arabic and it provides religious instruction in Islam or Christianity, as well as the Druze religion. The Compulsory Education Law has substantially changed the traditional Arab attitude towards formal education, especially of girls, almost all of whom attend school until the age of 16 (as compared with only 20% in 1948/49).

In 1986/87 there were some 67,000 students at Israel's seven universities. These include the Hebrew University of Jerusalem with almost 17,000 students, the Technion-Israel Institute of Technology with 9,000 students, Tel Aviv University (opened in 1956) with 19,400 stu-

Elementary school pupils studying in their modern classroom.

In this religious school, pupils divide their time between religious and secular subjects. Here they are studying the Talmud.

High-school students research their essays in the school library.

Library of the Islamic Museum, Jerusalem.

Yeshiva (religious academy) students studying in their library.

(top and center)
Students at ORT vocational
schools receive practical training
in their future occupations.

On the way to classes at an ORT
school.

A miniature kitchen introduces young children to the domestic arts.

Students at an ORT vocational school learn dressmaking.

Break time for students at Midreshet Sde Boker in the Negev. The complex, founded on the initiative of David Ben-Gurion, provides both general and vocational education and includes a teachers' training college and a field school.

dents, Bar-Ilan University (opened in 1955) with 9,500 students, Haifa University with 6,500 students, the Ben-Gurion University of the Negev (opened in 1969) with over 5,000 students and the Weizmann Institute of Science with 570 students.

Scientific Research

In the area of science, despite its small size, Israel has maintained a high level of research in most scientific fields and encouraged the establishment of centers of research around outstanding scientists. As in most developed countries, the industrial sector in Israel performs the bulk of research, but about one half of the government's investments in this area is allocated to the universities. It is here that most of the basic research and training of Israel's scientific manpower is concentrated. The major institutions of learning are represented on national policy-making bodies and thus play a pivotal role in influencing the shape and success of national science goals. At first, the universities conducted mainly basic research, but in recent years they have intensified their applied research activities. All the universities now have research authorities coordinating and directing the application of research results and promoting the exchange between the university and industry. Relative to the size of its labor force, Israel has more authors publishing in the natural sciences, engineering, agriculture and medicine, and also in the social sciences and humanities, than any other country. (Israel has 58.4% of the total publishing authors in academic fields per 10,000 labor force, while Switzerland has 36.1%, USA 33.2%, UK 28.2% and France 21%).

The high level of Israeli scientific research has been maintained due to efforts to integrate Israeli science into the international scientific community. Post-doctoral research posts and sabbaticals abroad are encouraged, as well as attendance at scientific conferences. Israel is an important center for international scientific conferences, serving as the host to well over 100 such gatherings annually. In addition, a large proportion of Israel's research community is made up of immigrant scien-

Inaugural ceremony of the Weizmann Institute of Science, Rehovot, in 1949.

tists who have maintained and fostered their overseas ties even after their arrival in Israel.

In addition to the research being carried out at institutes of learning, funds have been allocated to government research institutes and to over 50 research and development funds administered by various ministries, public institutions and foundations in all areas of scientific research.

Literature, Theater, Music and Art

Israel has renewed its claim to the name "People of the Book" by its very active literary and publishing community. The country ranks among the top in the world for the number of titles published in proportion to the population. In 1984/85 over 4,100 titles were published. Of these more than 750 were literary works, including original Hebrew

Advanced construction technology has allowed the architect to respond to the fast-evolving needs of science in this unconventional building which houses the Koffler Accelerator at the Weizmann Institute, Rehovot.

Simone de Beauvoir receiving the Jerusalem Prize for literature from Mayor Teddy Kollek at the 1975 Jerusalem International Book Fair.

Publishers from all over the world meet and exhibit their wares at the International Book Fair which takes place in Jerusalem every two years.

A booth shared by an American and an Israeli publisher at the Jerusalem International Book Fair.

books and translations into Hebrew from other languages. Other fields include the humanities (325), social sciences (200), Judaism and other religions (180) and childrens' books (174).

Among the distinguished Israeli writers in Hebrew are such authors as the late S. Y. Agnon, winner of the 1966 Nobel Prize for Literature, Amos Oz, A. B. Yehoshua, David Shahar, Amos Elon and Ephraim Kishon. There are also Israeli writers of note in Arabic, English, Russian and other languages.

There are approximately 1,000 public libraries throughout the country, including mobile libraries which serve outlying communities and neighborhoods in large cities. In 1986/87 about half of the population

Winners of the 1987 Israel Prize, given each year for outstanding contributions to Israeli cultural life in different fields.

The control room at Kol Israel (the Voice of Israel) radio broadcasting station.

aged 14 and over read one or more books each month. Every other year the Jerusalem International Book Fair brings hundreds of foreign publishers to the country. An annual Hebrew Book Week takes place in every city in Israel, with books for sale at reduced prices on open stalls. Since 1976 there has also been an annual Arabic Book Week in Haifa and other towns with large Arab populations.

The Israeli press is as diversified as the population. In 1985 there were 21 daily newspapers, 9 in Hebrew, 4 in Arabic and the remainder in other languages. In addition, there are some 900 periodicals of both general and specific interest, of which about 600 are in Hebrew.

Radio and television are controlled by the Israel Broadcasting

A program goes on the air at the studios of Galei Tzahal, the army radio station.

Authority, whose Board includes both public and government members. Kol Israel (the Voice of Israel) broadcasts on five internal radio stations and one international station daily. Popular music, classical music, "spoken word" programs and news are the major fields of these stations. The Arabic language station broadcasts 18 hours a day. The overseas network broadcasts around the world on the short wave in 16 languages. The IDF radio — "Galei Tzahal" — broadcasts 24 hours a day.

Television broadcasts are divided between educational programs during the day, children's and Arabic programs in the afternoon and evening, and general Hebrew programs. About half of the programs are locally produced. Most Hebrew programs are subtitled in Arabic and vice-versa, while English programs carry subtitles in both languages. In 1987 a second channel began experimental broadcasting. This channel is planned as a private one which will carry advertising.

Television coverage of basketball, one of Israel's most popular sports.

Opposite page:
(top)
The Israel Song Festival takes place in Jerusalem on Independence Day.
(bottom)
Opening of the International Folklore Festival in Haifa.

First steps in ballet.

The famous Galina Valery Panov dances at the Mann Auditorium, Tel Aviv, in 1977.

Five major theatrical repertory groups perform a wide range of original works in Hebrew as well as translations of the entire range of classical and contemporary drama. The companies are the Habimah, Israel's National Theater which was originally established in Moscow in 1917 and moved to Palestine in 1928; the Cameri, the Tel Aviv Municipal Theater (established in 1944), the Haifa Municipal Theater (1961), the Beersheba Municipal Theater (1974) and the Jerusalem Khan Theater. Although each is based in a major city, the companies travel and perform throughout the country. There are also numerous smaller groups including a kibbutz theater, two mime groups, English and Arabic groups.

Music and dance are among the most popular Israeli activities and it is therefore not surprising that a large number of orchestras, ensembles, choirs and dance groups perform regularly. The foremost of these is the Israel Philharmonic Orchestra, under the direction of maestro Zubin

Leonard Bernstein conducting an open-air concert of the Israel Philharmonic Orchestra in 1948.

Mehta. Founded in 1936, it presents more than 150 concerts a year in Israel and frequently undertakes overseas tours, performing with world-renowned conductors and soloists. The Jerusalem Symphony Orchestra of the Israel Broadcasting Authority pays special attention to local composers and performers at its regular concerts. Other groups include the Haifa, Beersheba, Netanya, and Ramat Gan Orchestras, the Israel Chamber Orchestra and the Tel Aviv and Rinat Choirs.

The Inbal Dance Theater, founded in 1949, concentrates on ethnic and traditional motifs. Batsheva, Bat-Dor and the Kibbutz Dance Companies perform modern and classical works. The Kol U'Demama (Sound and Silence) dance ensemble is composed of both deaf and hearing dancers with the latter giving visual signs to the former to indicate rhythm and pace.

A variety of these and other performances are concentrated in regular festivals, held in addition to the usual seasonal performances. The Israel Festival in Jerusalem presents outstanding international and local artists and groups each summer. The Ein Gev Music Festival is held every spring on the shores of the Sea of Galilee, and the recently inaugurated Tel Aviv Spring Festival has proved to be immensely popular. Festivals of jazz, children's songs, Hassidic melodies, liturgica and choral music are some of the other cultural events which take place annually.

The more than 80 museums in Israel recorded over 8 million visits in 1984/85. Their collections include items in such fields as archeology, history, art, Judaica, ethnology and folklore, science technology, and zoology. Among the largest are the Israel Museum in Jerusalem which incorporates the Bezalel Museum of Jewish Art and the Shrine of the Book which houses the Dead Sea Scrolls; the Tel Aviv Museum; Beit Hatefutzot, the Museum of the Jewish Diaspora; the Ha'aretz Museum in Tel Aviv which includes the Lasky Planetarium; and the Institute for Islamic Art in Jerusalem.

The Shrine of the Book, built to house the Dead Sea Scrolls at the Israel Museum in Jerusalem, was designed in the form of the lids of the ancient clay vessels in which the scrolls were kept.

The beginning of modern art in Israel can be dated back to the founding of the Bezalel School of Art and Design in Jerusalem in 1906. Today, in addition to the active Bezalel School, there are artists' colonies in Safed, Ein Hod and Old Jaffa. Galleries throughout the country sell the works of both internationally famous and local artists, some of whom have also developed a world-wide name.

Films and Sports

In 1986 nineteen full-length films were produced in Israel, some of which were Israeli, some foreign, and others co-productions. Local film production began in 1960 and has expanded from the purely local market to export for viewing abroad. The Israel Film Center promotes the production of foreign films in Israel. The Jerusalem Cinematheque, with its unique Film Archive, sponsors an annual Film Festival, offers regular screenings of classic movies and collects, catalogues and preserves films dealing with Jewish themes or aspects of Jewish life.

Israel's most popular sports are soccer (football) and basketball. It has four major national sports organizations Maccabi (1912), Betar (1924), Hapoel (1926), Elitzur (1939). The victory of the Tel Aviv Maccabi Basketball Team in the 1977 and 1981 European Cup established the country's place in the sporting world. Other sports include tennis (whose centers all over Israel have become increasingly popular among youth and adults), swimming, athletics, sailing, weight-lifting and volleyball. Soccer and basketball league games, on the local, regional and national levels, are attended by thousands of loyal fans. The Wingate Institute of Physical Education and Sports trains physical education teachers, physiotherapists, coaches and instructors and has departments for research, sports and medicine. Annual functions such as the Jerusalem March and the swim across the Sea of Galilee attract hundreds of visitors from abroad as well as thousands of Israelis.

Swimming pool at the Haifa Technion.

Members of a youth movement set up their summer camp.

Balancing beam excercise.

Gymnastic display at Wingate Institute of Physical Culture near Netanya. The institute, run by the Ministry of Education and Culture, comprises a college for physical education teachers, a school for physiotherapists, a course for coaches, and a school for physical training instructors of the Israel Defense Forces.

Health and welfare

When the first Jewish pioneers arrived in Palestine toward the end of the 19th century, they found a land ridden with disease. Malaria, enteric fever, typhoid and dysentery took a heavy toll of Jews and Arabs every year. Infant mortality struck down numerous children before they reached their first birthday. Trachoma and ringworm were widespread, as were many other infectious diseases.

Although a number of Jewish clinics in Jerusalem (Bikur Holim established in 1843, Misgav Ladach in 1888 and Sha'arei Zedek in 1902) served the Jewish, Muslim and Christian population of that city and surroundings, they were not sufficient for the new settlements established by the Zionists. Therefore, in 1912 a regional association of agricultural workers in Judea established their own health service, Kupat Holim, the Workers' Sick Fund. Beginning with a single doctor and a nurse, the original aim of the Fund was to bring medical care to all the cooperative villages, collective settlements and kibbutzim in the new Jewish agrarian areas of the country. In 1920, after the founding of the Histadrut (the General Federation of Labor), the Fund became part of the new organization, providing medical care to all its members and soon spreading its services to the towns as well as the villages.

The second health service established by the pioneers was the Hadassah Medical Service. In 1913 Hadassah, the Women's Zionist Organization of America, sent trained nurses to Jerusalem to provide pre- and post-natal care. Five years later the American Zionist Medical Unit,

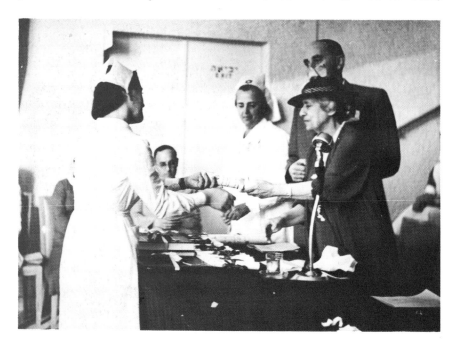

Henrietta Szold, founder of Hadassah, presenting diplomas to nurses in the early 1930s.

sponsored by Hadassah and the Joint Distribution Committee, arrived in the country. Consisting of 44 doctors, nurses, sanitary engineers and dentists, the Unit set up modern hospitals in Haifa, Jaffa, Jerusalem, Safed and Tiberias and opened a School of Nursing in Jerusalem. It established a network of mother-and-child care stations in many parts of the country and initiated school hygiene and lunch programs in Jerusalem.

During the Mandatory period these two organizations grew and expanded. The immigrants who arrived before 1948 were usually young and healthy with high standards of hygiene and there were many physicians or health specialists. The British Administration concentrated on malaria and smallpox control. Thus, by 1948 when Israel was established, the health standards of its population were quite high. Malaria had been wiped out, inoculations against smallpox and typhoid were given to all children, and infant mortality had dropped to a very low rate.

However, the newly established Ministry of Health was quickly faced with a crisis. Many of the thousands of immigrants who poured

Hadassah mother and child welfare station in the Old City of Jerusalem in the 1920s.

Opposite page:
(top)
A visiting Hadassah nurse bandages pupils at a school in the Old City of Jerusalem in 1936.
(bottom)
Kupat Holim (Sick Fund) clinic in 1950.

In the early 1920s, milk was distributed to mothers by Hadassah's Tipat Halav *(in Hebrew, "a drop of milk") service from the back of a donkey.*

into the country were survivors of the concentration camps and broken in body. Others suffered from diseases that had almost been eradicated or had never taken hold in the country. Of a group of 45,000 Yemenite Jews, for example, who arrived in 1949, there were 20,000 carriers of bilharzia, 27,000 cases of trachoma, 20,000 of malaria, 8,000 of tropical ulcer, and many of active tuberculosis. Still other immigrants lacked the most elementary knowledge of hygiene.

The Ministry met the challenge by recruiting personnel, hospitalizing the severe cases and setting up health care centers in the transit camps. After 1954 it instituted health examinations of immigrants before their arrival in Israel.

Today the Ministry is the supreme administrative and coordinating health authority in the country. It controls medical standards, licenses medical personnel and supervises the planning and construction of hospitals. It also provides direct patient services through government owned and operated hospitals and mother-and-child care centers, and school health programs.

About 95% of the population is covered by voluntary mutual health insurance operated by a number of Health Funds. The Funds provide hospitalization, treatment at clinics or at a physician's office, dental and optical care, medicines and convalescent facilities. Employees are legally required to financially participate in their worker's health insurance.

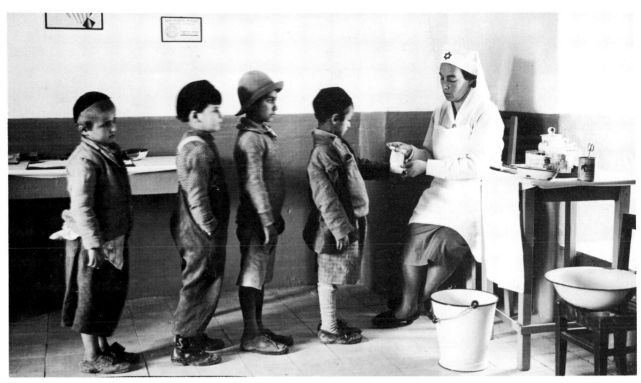

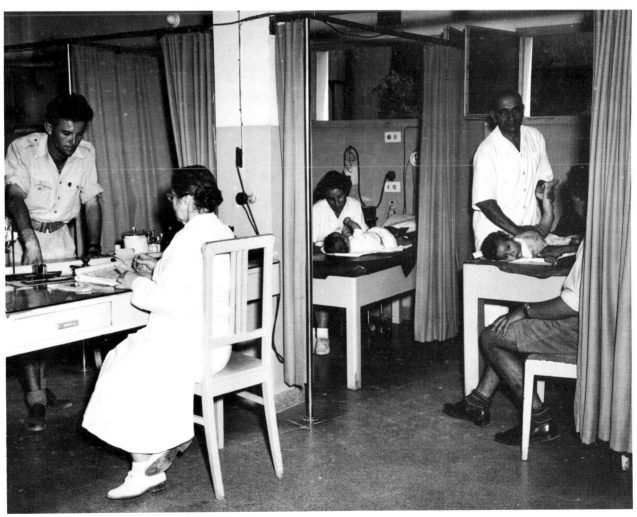

Children's ward at Rothschild Hospital in the Old City, Jerusalem, in 1939.

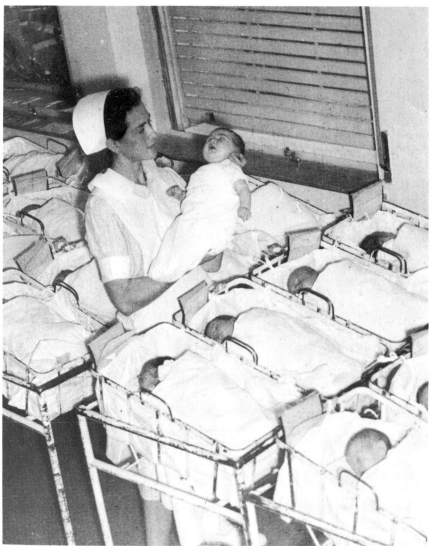

Children born at Beilinson Hospital, Petach Tikva, within the week of the Proclamation of Independence of the State of Israel.

The mother-and-child care centers of Hadassah and other voluntary organizations were transferred to the government or local municipalities over the years. Hadassah is still a major factor in the country's health through Hadassah in Jerusalem, with two hospitals at Mt. Scopus and Ein Karem, as well as schools of medicine, nursing, dentistry and pharamacology. Other organizations, mostly volunteer, include the Magen David Adom (corresponding to the Red Cross), Malben-Joint (aged, chronically ill and mental patients), Ilan (Israel Foundation for Handicapped Children), Alyn (orthopedic hospital and rehabilitation center for children), the Cancer Association, the Anti-Tuberculosis League and many others.

As a result of improved health care infant death rates among Jews in Israel has dropped from 39.2 in 1951 to 11.4 in 1986, and from 48.8 in 1951 to 18.6 in 1986 for non-Jews. Life expectancy has increased to 73.5 years for males (as compared to 65.2 in 1949) and 77 years for females (67.9 in 1949). The number of hospitals has grown from 66 in 1948 to 150 in 1986, of which 40% were privately owned, some 20% government owned, and 10% owned by Kupat Holim. The number of beds increased to over 27,000 in 1986, as compared to 4,600 in 1948, a rate of 6.32 per 1,000 population. In 1982 there were over 900 mother-and-child health centers throughout the country, 60% run by the government and 30% by the General Kupat Holim. The approximately 10,000 physicians in the country make Israel's rate of doctors to the population one of the highest in the world. There are over 20,000 nurses, about half of whom are registered nurses.

Medical research is well developed in a number of centers through-

Premature babies' service at Tel Hashomer Hospital, near Tel Aviv, 1985.

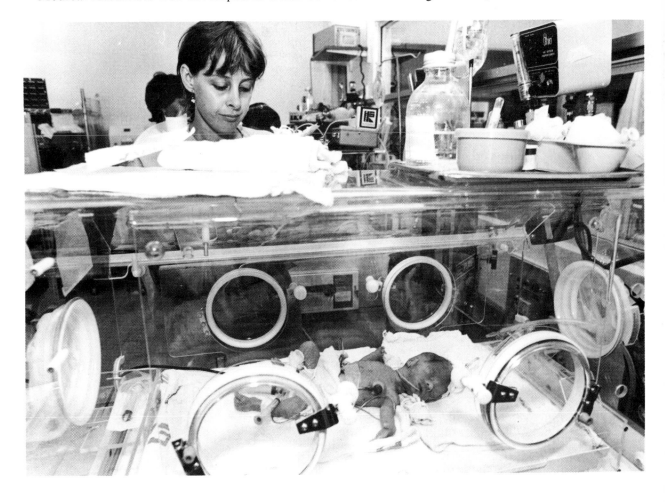

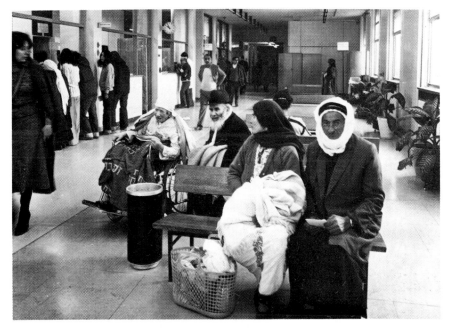

Opposite page:
(top)
Hadassah Medical Center at Ein Karem.
(bottom)
Hadassah Hospital on Mount Scopus, Jerusalem.

Outpatients' waiting hall at Hadassah Medical Center, Ein Karem.

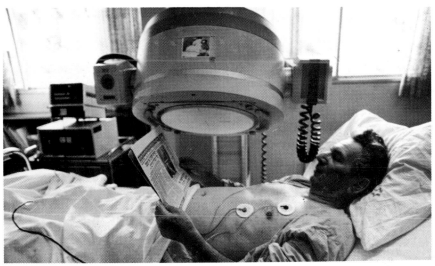

Computerized scanner at Beilinson Hospital, Petach Tikva.

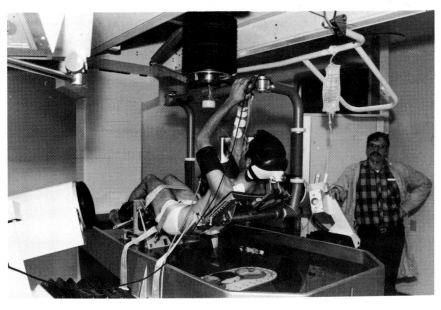

New treatment with a lithotripter which eliminates kidney stones and saves the patient going through surgery.

Diploma presentation ceremony at the Hadassah Nursing School, 1949.

(right)
Graduation ceremony for students of public health and community medicine, 1979.

out Israel with impressive advances made in such fields as cancer, immunology, cardiology, surgery and the treatment and rehabilitation of burn, war and accident victims.

Social Welfare

Israel is a welfare state committed to combating want among its citizens and helping those in distress. It has established a ramified network of legislation, insurance and services for this purpose, which are among the most advanced and liberal in the world.

Under the British Mandate workmen's compensation was the only legislation which affected a large number of workers, but even that law only applied to manual laborers in certain trades. With the establishment of the State it was decided to institute a comprehensive system of social security. In 1954 the National Insurance Law established the National Insurance Institute (*Bituach Leumi*) which collects contributions from employers, employees and individuals, and administers the various benefits, which presently include: old age pension paid to men

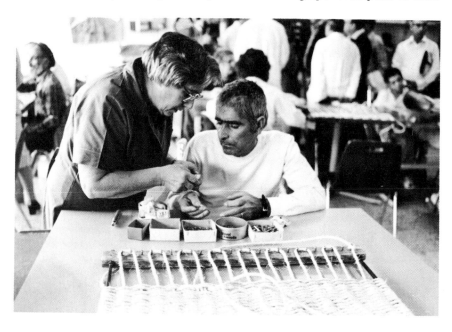

Occupational therapy at Beit Levinstein Rehabilitation Center.

from the age of 70 and to women from the age of 65; if their income falls below a certain minimum, these pensions are paid five years earlier to both men and women. In 1986/87 over 310,000 persons received old age pensions and an additional 90,000 received survivors' pensions paid to the widow or widower of the insured. In addition, the Institute covers the cost of burial with a grant made directly to the burial society.

Work injuries insurance covers all employees and self-employed persons, as well as members of cooperatives. Payments include daily injury benefits (nearly 58,000 in 1986/7), permanent disability pensions (over 10,000) and survivors' benefits (3,300) to the dependents of a person fatally injured in a work accident.

General disability payment was first implemented in 1974 for those unable to support themselves because of a physical, mental or psychological limitation from birth, as a result of sickness or accident. Some 68,000 general disability payments were made in 1986/87, as well as 4,500 payments for those who are dependent on the help of others, 11,000 payments for the purchase of a vehicle to persons of limited mobility and 4,200 payments for the benefit of disabled children.

Maternity benefits include a birth grant, part of which is paid directly to the hospital to cover delivery expenses and the rest as a cash payment to the mother, as well as an allowance for up to 12 weeks of maternity leave at 75% of the mother's average wage. In 1986/87 nearly 100,000 maternity grants were paid and over 40,000 maternity allowances.

The guarantee of alimony payments went into effect in 1972 and 8,500 payments, as determined by court decisions, were made in 1986/87.

The new Sha'arei Zedek Hospital, Jerusalem.

Minister of Health Shoshana Arbeli-Almoslino cuts the cake at the Hadassah diamond jubilee celebrations in 1987.

Unemployment benefits were paid to 58,600 persons in 1986/87 and income support benefits for those who have no income or whose income falls short of the minimum level were paid to 31,500 persons.

Since 1975 a child allowance was paid by the Institute for every child under 18 years of age. However, in 1985 the "first child" allowance was discontinued for families with three children or less. Some 508,000 families received a child allowance in 1986/87.

The Ministry of Labor and Social Affairs maintains an extensive network of rehabilitation services, community facilities and programs for youth, adults and the aged. It runs day-care centers and coordinates adoption procedure and foster home placement. It supervises the social workers attached to almost every school in the country, conducts youth rehabilitation programs, provides probation services and runs temporary shelters for juvenile offenders. It provides workshops for the physically and mentally handicapped, drug and alcohol rehabilitation programs, home nursing for the aged and "meals-on-wheels," as well as a variety of programs at local community centers for persons of all ages.

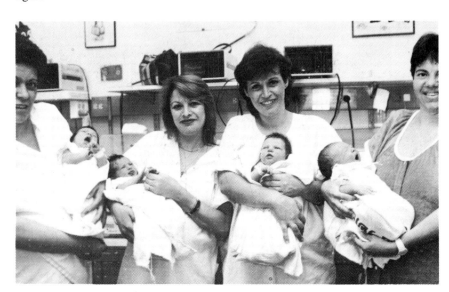

Four proud mothers show off their newborn "test tube" babies all born within 24 hours on the same weekend in 1987 as a result of in vitro fertilization at Hadassah Medical Center at Ein Karem.

Some 250 private voluntary organizations supplement the work of the Ministry. Among these are the JDC-Malben whose programs care for the sick, aged and handicapped immigrants; ORT (Organization for Rehabilitation through Training) which runs the country's largest network of technical and vocational education; Mo'etzet Hapo'alot (Womens' Workers Council) which maintains kindergartens, day-care centers, clubs and summer camps, vocational and argricultural schools, community centers and clubs for Arab women; WIZO (Women's International Zionist Organization) which has day-care centers, youth clubs, agricultural and vocational schools, rest homes, home industries and gift shops; Mizrachi Women-Emunah which maintains a children's village, vocational schools, and agricultural schools, and youth centers; Hadassah which runs a comprehensive high school, a vocational center and a college to train ex-servicemen and others in the medical and technical fields.

Magen Davi. ↗dom headquarters in Tel Aviv.

Animal health is not neglected in Israel. Here veterinaries are treating a baby camel.

Geography

The Land of Israel lies at the southwest tip of the Asian continent, between the Mediterranean Sea on the west, the Syrian and Arabian deserts on the east and southeast, and the Red Sea in the south. In the north, the lower courses of the Litani River and the Hermon Mountain range form the natural boundary of the Land.

Because of its location at the crossroads between Asia and Africa, throughout history the Land has served as a vital trade route and bridge between the two continents. As a result it has been the object of both imperial ambitions and conquest.

Despite its natural frontiers, the borders of the Land of Israel were never static. They expanded and contracted depending upon the power of the country's ruler. Similarly, since its establishment the State of Israel has never known permanent borders. Until 1967 its boundaries were the temporary armistice lines set forth in the Armistice Agreement signed with Jordan, Lebanon, Syria and Egypt in 1949. Since 1967 the eastern border of the country has, in effect, been the Jordan River, with the West Bank under Israeli control, based on the cease-fire agreement with Jordan. The northeastern border is defined by a Separation-of-Forces Agreement with Syria, signed in May 1974, with the Golan Heights annexed by Israel in 1981. The northern border remains as defined by the 1949 agreement with Lebanon, although the

View of the coast at Ashkelon.

Israeli Army assists the South Lebanese Army within a security zone running some 10 miles north of the border. Only in the south-west is there a permanent border, as defined by the 1979 Israel–Egypt Peace Treaty. The total area within these borders is 27,800 sq. km., or 10,735 square miles.

Although the country is small, it contains every type of geographical terrain and is generally described in terms of four major regions — the Coastal Plain, the Western Mountain Zone, the Rift Valley and the Transjordanian Plateau.

The Coastal Plain
The length of the Mediterranean coast, from the Sinai Desert in the south to Lebanon in the north, is approximately 270 km (170 miles). The southern part of the coastline — from El Arish to Tel Aviv — is almost straight, with breaks at Gaza and Ashkelon. Its long sandy beaches are covered by quartz sand from the Nile Delta and the Sinai coast. The northern coastal zone is indented at several points, although only at Haifa is there a true bay. The inland mountains border on the sea, with the cliffs reaching a maximum height of 40 m. (130 ft.) at Netanya. The beaches are therefore poorly developed, existing only around coastal indentations.

The Jordan River.

Throughout history the coastal plain has been the most densely populated and intensively cultivated area of the country. Today, the region contains almost two-thirds of Israel's population. The Galilee and Haifa plains contain most of the country's heavy industry and its largest port. The Carmel Plain, further south, is the site of resort towns, while the Sharon Plain is dominated by Tel Aviv and its various satellite cities, the center of Israel's economy, business and banking. The Judean Plain contains the cities of Ashdod and Ashkelon, with port services and industry. The Southern Plain, known as the Gaza Strip since 1948, is some 40 km. long and 5–10 km. wide (25×3–6 miles) and is closest to the desert, both in location and character.

The Plain of Jezreel.

Granite gorge in the Negev, near Eilat.

The Mountains

Extending the entire length of the country, the Western Mountain Zone is often referred to as the "backbone" of the Cisjordan. It is the southernmost tip of the Great Alpines and of medium height. The forest and terraces which once covered its slopes have given way to brush and thorn.

The Negev Highlands, including the Eilat Mountains, are a continuation of the mountainous region of the Sinai Desert. Outcrops of Nubian sandstone in the Negev have resulted in such spectacular features as Solomon's Pillars, north of Eilat, and the Red Canyon, deeply incised in multicolored sandstone. The Highlands also contain wide, elongated valley-like basins.

The Central Mountain Range extends from Beersheba to the Jezreel Valley. The section known as the Judean Hills is some 80 km. (50 miles) long and runs almost continuously along the watershed. Characterized by intensively terraced slopes, it is subdivided into the Hebron Mountains, where the city of Hebron is located, the Jerusalem Mountains, site of Jerusalem, Israel's capital, with the Mount of Olives, the Mount Scopus ridge, and the Bet-El Mountains which contain the main road from the Coastal Plain to Jerusalem. The Samarian section links the Judean Hills with the Galilean range. It contains the biblically famous peaks of Ebal and Gerizim and Mount Gilboa.

Mount Tabor, isolated from the other mountains, rises abruptly from the Jezreel Valley to an altitude of about 560 m. (1840 ft.).

The Mountains of Upper Galilee rise to 1,208 m. (3,963 ft.) at Meron. Their plentiful rain, fresh springs and fertile valleys have enabled the farming villages to produce fruit, olives and cotton, and carp in artificial ponds. Lower down, the Galilee Mountains are half as high with Mount Carmel rising to 546 m. (1,790 ft.), its slopes luxuriant in vegetation.

Mount Hermon, whose several peaks rise above Israel, Lebanon and Syria to a height of 2,814 m. (9,230 ft.), towers above the basalt plateau of the Golan Heights which, in turn, overlooks the farming villages of the Hula and Jordan Valleys. The Hermon is the only region in the country with a true mountainous climate, a snow-cap, heavy rain, blizzards and ski slopes.

Snow-capped Mount Hermon.

The Valleys

The Rift Valley, part of the great Syrian–African Rift some 6,000 km. (3,730 miles) long, extends from Eilat in the south to the sources of the Jordan in the north. The Jordan River runs throughout the entire length of the Valley, from the Sea of Galilee and to the Dead Sea. The Valley has very little precipitation in the southern and central areas, gradually increasing northward, and finally reaching sub-humid levels north of the Sea of Galilee.

Just south of the Jordan River headwaters, including the Dan and Banias Rivers, is the Hula Basin, formed by lava flows descending from the Golan Heights. The runoff waters of the Hula Lake covered the surrounding area with marshy swamps. Jewish pioneers began to reclaim the swamps in the 1930s, uncovering rich soil, and when the project was completed in 1958, the Lake was also drained. Today the Hula is one of the most intensively cultivated areas in the country; farms, fruit orchards, cotton fields and fish ponds cover the region.

South of the Hula Basin is the Sea of Galilee and the Plain of Ginnosar, also known as the Vale of Capernaum. Further south lies the Jordan Valley, some 105 km. (65 miles) in length. The riverbed of the Jordan is covered with dense forests and walled-in by steep gullied slopes. Tributaries of the Jordan have created wide valleys to the west of the River, including the Beisan (Beth She'an) Valley, which extend far into the eastern parts of the Judean and Samarian Mountains. The Valley is mainly semi-arid, but the northern section is extremely fertile with sub-tropical fruits prevalent.

From the Dead Sea to the Gulf of Eilat is the Arava Valley, characterized by flash floods, salty waters and marshy earth. The Valley is

The plains and hills of Samaria.

today being developed for intensive agriculture by the use of desalinization methods.

The Jezreel Valley, also known as the Plain of Armageddon and the Plain of Esdralon, lies between the Mediterranean and the Rift Valley, separating Mount Tabor and Givat Hamoreh, which reach heights of over 500 m. (1,640 ft.) above sea level. In the past, the run-off rain from the mountains and the poor soil turned large parts of the Valley into swamps. Now, after the marshes have been drained and the endemic malaria eradicated, the Valley, which spreads over 365 sq. km. (140 sq. miles), has become Israel's major granary.

View of the Hula Valley with Mount Hermon in the background.

Aerial view of Megiddo and the Valley of Megiddo.

The Judean Desert.
(right)
Nature reserve park at Ein Gedi.

Swiftly-flowing Wadi Qelt sustains a strip of lush vegetation in the arid Judean Desert.

The Deserts

The Negev Desert comprises almost two-thirds of the area of Israel. Comprised of low sandstone hills, steppes and loess plains in the north, and bare rocky peaks, craters, and lofty mountain plateaus in the south, much of the land is being reclaimed by irrigation.

The Judean Desert, located between the Judean Mountains and the Dead Sea, has throughout history been a desolate refuge for fugitives and a place of solitude for hermits and zealots. Its numerous canyons and valleys, interspersed with flat-topped hills, receive little rain because of the massive hills which intercept the rain-bearing winds.

Masada and Herodium are located here, two ancient fortresses which served the Jews in their battles against the Romans, as well as the town of Jericho, an oasis of palms and green in the midst of the wilderness.

The thorny acacia tree flourishes on the sparsely vegetated shores of the Dead Sea.
(left)
View of the Dead Sea.

Rivers and Seas
The longest of Israel's rivers is the Jordan. Flowing along some 250 km. (155 miles) it descends some 700 m. (2,297 ft.) to the Dead Sea, the steep drop accounting for its name (*yored* "to descend" in Hebrew). The Jordan begins on Mount Hermon where its three main headwaters — the Dan, Banias and Hasbani — are fed from spring waters, rainfall

View of Judea with Bethlehem and Herodion in the Judean Desert in the background.

Waterfall at Banias.

(right)
The Banias, one of the sources of the Jordan River.

and melting snow. The three headwaters merge just above the Hula Basin from where the Jordan River makes its way into the northern tip of the Sea of Galilee. It then emerges and winds for more than 100 km. (62 miles) to the Dead Sea. During this course it receives additional impetus from a number of tributaries, including the Yarmuk River from Transjordan, the Jabbok and the Arava Rivers.

The Dead Sea is some 80 km. long and 17 km. (50×10½ miles) wide — a total of 1,000 sq. km. (386 sq.miles) in area. Some 400 m. (1,312 ft.) below the level of the Mediterranean, it is the lowest point on earth. Because it has no outlet to the sea and the water flowing into it is balanced by the evaporation from its surface, the Dead Sea has a salt concentration of over 25%, making it so dense that one cannot sink in it. Magnesium, potassium, sodium, calcium chloride and magnesium bro-

Two views of the Jordan River.

Salt mounds float on the surface of the Dead Sea where the salinity of the water is sometimes four times that of the ocean.

(left)
The Sea of Galilee.

One of the springs at Tabgha on the shore of the Sea of Galilee.

mide are extracted from the sea by the Dead Sea Works Company, located on the south-western shore at the site of the biblical city of Sodom. Also along this shore are numerous hotels for those seeking the beneficial effects of the Dead Sea's mineral waters and thermal springs, in addition to a series of nature reserves and the Kibbutz Ein Gedi.

Israel's other inland sea is the Sea of Galilee also known as Lake Kinneret (*kinnor* — "harp" in Hebrew) or Lake Tiberias. About 170 sq. km. (65½ sq. miles) in area, the Sea of Galilee is fed by the Jordan River and underground springs. Numerous hot mineral springs surround it and it supplies most of Israel's fresh water fish.

Israel utilizes almost 95% of its extremely limited water resources. Before the establishment of the State, these resources were poorly developed with only 50,000 acres (out of a potential of one million acres) under irrigation. The country's small annual rainfall, underground water and river water (mainly from the Jordan) are concentrated in the northeast, while the demand for them is in the center and south. In 1964 Israel completed the National Water Carrier which brings water from the Sea of Galilee to the rest of the country through 130 km. (81 miles) of pipes, aqueducts, reservoirs, tunnels and dams. The National Carrier is linked to the Yarkon project which supplies water to the Negev and some twenty regional projects draw water from the National Carrier to different locations. Desalinization, trickle irrigation and the management of groundwater, flood flows and rainfall run-off are other methods now being used to increase the utilization and effectiveness of Israel's water.

Climate

Israel's location between the arid subtropical zone of Egypt and the wet subtropical zone of Lebanon explains the great contrast between the light rainfall in the south and the heavy rainfall in the north. Rain normally falls during the months of November to April with three-quarters of the seasonal rainfall occurring in December, January and February.

The highest temperatures in the country are in the Rift Valley, while the lowest are in the Upper Galilee. Relative humidity is higher near the coast; the Coastal Plain has hot, humid summers and mild winters; the hill regions have temperate summers and cool winters in the north and center, and hot and dry summers and warm winters in the south; the desert and Jordan Valley have mild winters and subtropical summers.

Heat waves, known as *hamsin* or *sharav*, usually occur in May, June, October and November, when the temperature rises (sometimes to body heat) and the humidity drops.

In the autumn, dry thistle heads and gathering clouds herald the approach of the rainy season.

Flora and Fauna

Israel's 3,000 species of flora make it one of the richest and most varied in the world. The 700 genera, belonging to 115 families, are a product of the region's landscape, the diversity of its topography and climate and the fact that it is a meeting place of different physical and geographic areas.

The most ancient of the country's plants are probably its olive trees. The grove in the Garden of Gethsemane, on Jerusalem's Mount of Olives, for example, is thought to date back to the period of the Second Temple. The oak, common throughout Israel, is mentioned in Genesis, in connection with Abraham's first home in the land.

Other trees include the pine, especially prevalent in the Jerusalem region; the Judas tree, whose lilac flowers adorn the mountains in the Spring; the carob, which grows on the slopes of the Carmel and Judean mountains, and the storax with trunks up to 6 m. (19½ ft.) in diameter and heights of up to 20 m. (65½ ft.), as well as the pomegranate, mulberry, acacia, fig, sycamore and palm trees. In the 40 years since the State was declared, more than 100 million trees have been planted on over 100,000 acres as part of the program of land reclamation and reafforestatation.

Israel has also developed some 28 parks under the supervision of the National Parks Authority and 280 nature reserves, covering nearly

(left to right)
Date palms; an ancient olive tree; a sycamore.

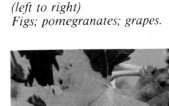

(left to right)
Figs; pomegranates; grapes.

Overleaf:
(clockwise from left)
*Wild flowers of Israel: A recent dis-
covery in the Negev, the Spafford
Sternbergia, thought previously to
grow only in the Mediterranean
zone; the Mariae iris in the sand
of the northern Negev; throughout the winter the Cyclamen,
white or pink, flowers in the
mountains of the Mediterranean
zone; a member of the orchid
family, the Helleborine grows
from the northern mountains to
the ravines of the Judean desert;
the Anemone blooms all over the
country for five months of the year.*

Opposite page:
(top)
*A young ibex scans the desert
from a vantage point.*
(bottom)
*The prickly pear, or sabra, has
given its name to native-born
Israelis because of the sweetness
of its fruits, protected by a
prickly exterior.*

(top right on this page)
*Sheep grazing beneath olive trees
on a carpet of spring flowers.*

*Even in the age of the automo-
bile, the camel has not lost its
importance to the Beduin of the
Negev.*

400,000 acres, of which 20 are open to the public with visitors' centers,
hiking trails and picnic areas.

The country's fauna is comprised of some 80 reptile and 70 mammal
species, and two wildlife reserves have been established to reintroduce
into Israel animals mentioned in the Bible and other extinct species.
Some 350 species of birds are either indigenous or stop over in Israel
on their way from Europe to Africa in the winter. These include eagles,
ospreys and vultures.

Index